POETRY AND LANGUAGE

POETRY AND LANGUAGE

Edited by **Brian Kellow**
London Board of Education
London, Ontario

John Krisak
London Board of Education
London, Ontario

MCGRAW-HILL RYERSON LIMITED
Toronto, Montreal, New York, St. Louis, San Francisco, Auckland, Bogotá, Guatemala, Hamburg, Lisbon, London, Madrid, Mexico, New Delhi, Panama, Paris, San Juan, São Paulo, Singapore, Sydney, Tokyo

Poetry and Language

ISBN 0-07-548620-2

  4567890   210987

Printed and bound in Canada

A list of acknowledgements appears on pages 267-272. Every reasonable effort has been made to trace the ownership of copyrighted material and to make due acknowledgement. Any errors or omissions will be gladly rectified in future editions.

Canadian Cataloguing in Publication Data
Main entry under title:
Poetry and language

Includes indexes.

ISBN 0-07-548620-2

1. Poetry – Collections.   I. Kellow, Brian.
II. Krisak, John.

PN6101.P63   808.81   C83-094076-6

Preface

Poetry is language. The study of poetry is the study of language. The conjunction of poetry and language forms the basis of this book.

Through an organized approach to the elements of the poetic craft, the student will become more aware of the dynamics of language. The study of poetry is vital in itself; the method introduced in this book will enhance the students' own use of language as well as their appreciation of poetry. This book is designed to help students to become sensitive, knowledgeable, appreciative readers and articulate writers.

Each unit concentrates on one aspect of poetry. The questions which follow each selection are seminal, addressed to one or two aspects of the poem. They provide access to the interior structure of the poem without diminishing its content.

The poems within each unit progress from the readily accessible to those which are more complex in content and expression. This structure permits students of differing abilities and grade levels to develop a facility with each concept. While the arrangement of units may seem arbitrary, it has been found to work effectively with junior and senior students. However, the sequence is not intended to be prescriptive. Teachers and students are encouraged to choose any order suited to their own needs and wishes.

This text provides sufficient material to be used during two consecutive school years. We recommend that poetry not be taught as a "unit of study" segregated from the study of prose and dramatic literature. In order to build a meaningful appreciation of the structure and craft of language, poetry should be taught on a daily or frequent basis in short, concentrated lessons. Since each poem, with its related questions and activities, is essentially a short lesson, poetry and language can be taught extensively rather than intensively or thematically. The intention is that students be exposed to poetry and language over an extended time in short lessons that can be integrated into any English course.

While much of the material has been selected from the works of poets writing in English, translations of poems written in as many as eighteen other languages are included.

Students should have ample opportunity to write creatively and expressively in response to the poems in this collection. We believe that it is not enough to read poems and to answer questions about their content. For students to appreciate poetry and language, it is absolutely necessary that they become personally involved with the poem through thinking, speaking, and writing.

In memory of Pablo Neruda, we dedicate this book to our students.

Brian Kellow
John Krisak
London, Canada

Table of Contents

...for me you turned language
into a landslide of glass houses.

Master, companion,
you have shown me so many clear things
that wherever I am, you give me your clarity.

Pablo Neruda
from "To Acario Cotapos"

1 SOUND

"Listening..."

crickets...
then
thunder

Larry Wiggin

Questions:
1. What situation do these words suggest to you?
2. What similarities are there between crickets and thunder? What differences are there?
3. What is the difference between a sound and a noise?

Activities:
1. Say the word "crickets" so that it sounds like crickets.
2. Say the word "thunder" so that it sounds like thunder.
3. Compose several poems in the same form as Wiggin's poem.

Listening...
After a while,
I take up my axe again

Rod Wilmot

Questions:
1. What situation do these words suggest to you?
2. What do you know about the speaker?
3. Is this person listening **to** something or **for** something? How do you know?

Activities:
1. Remove the word "listening." How does its removal change the poem?
2. Remove the word "again." How does its removal change the poem?
3. Replace the word "axe" with a different word. How does your word alter the poem?
4. Remove the last line of the poem and substitute a line of your own invention.
5. Write a paragraph about the situation and events you envision in this poem.

Church Bells, Montreal

Against the hard
clear ring of the bells

measure that quick
whispered tick of our lives.

Raymond Souster

Questions:
1. *What two things are being compared?*
2. *What words suggest the sound of bells?*
3. *What words in the second stanza balance words in the first?*

Onomatopoeia is a device in which the sound of a word imitates the sound of the object to which it refers.

Activity:
1. *List all the words you can think of that imitate the sound of bells.*

The Watch

I wakened on my hot, hard bed,
Upon the pillow lay my head;
Beneath the pillow I could hear
My little watch was ticking clear.
I thought the throbbing of it went
Like my continual discontent;
I thought it said in every tick:
I am so sick, so sick, so sick;
O Death, come quick, come quick, come quick,
Come quick, come quick, come quick, come quick.

Frances Cornford

Questions:
1. *What do you know about the speaker? How do you know it?*
2. *Why does the poet use the word "throbbing" in line 5?*
3. *What contribution do rhyme, rhythm, and onomatopoeia make to the poem?*

Johnnie Crack and Flossie Snail

Johnnie Crack and Flossie Snail
Kept their baby in a milking pail
Flossie Snail and Johnnie Crack
One would pull it out and one would put it back

O it's my turn now said Flossie Snail
To take the baby from the milking pail
And it's my turn now said Johnnie Crack
To smack it on the head and put it back

Johnnie Crack and Flossie Snail
Kept their baby in a milking pail
One would put it back and one would pull it out
And all it had to drink was ale and stout
For Johnnie Crack and Flossie Snail
Always used to say that stout and ale
Was *good* for a baby in a milking pail.

Dylan Thomas

Activities:
1. *Read the poem silently.*
2. *Read the poem aloud and clap your hands to the rhythm.*
3. *Compose a four-line stanza with a regular rhyme scheme and rhythmical pattern.*

---

from The Kallyope Yell

Proud men
Eternally
Go about
Slander me,
call me the "Calliope,"
Sizz ...
Fizz ...

I am the Gutter Dream,
Tune-maker, born of steam,
Tooting joy, tooting hope.
I am the Kallyope,
Car called the Kallyope,
Willy willy willy wah HOO!
See the flags: snow-white tent,
See the bear and elephant,
See the monkey jump the rope,
Listen to the Kallyope, Kallyope, Kallyope!
Soul of the rhinoceros
And the hippopotamus
(Listen to the lion roar!)
Jaguar, cockatoot,
Loons, owls,
Hoot, Hoot.

Listen to the lion roar!
Listen to the lion *roar*,
Listen to the lion R-O-A-R!
Hear the leopard cry for gore,
Willy willy willy wah HOO!
Hail the bloody Indian band,
Hail, all hail the popcorn stand,
Hail to Barnum's picture there,
People's idol everywhere,
Whoop whoop whoop WHOOP!
Music of the mob am I,
Circus day's tremendous cry:-

I am the Kallyope, Kallyope, Kallyope!
Hoot toot, hoot toot, hoot toot, hoot toot,
Willy willy willy willy wah HOO!
Sizz . . .
Fizz . . .

Vachel Lindsay

Activities:
1. *Describe a calliope.*
2. *Prepare for a choral reading of the poem, experimenting with solo voices, paired voices, and quartets. Try varying the rhythm, pitch, and volume.*
3. *Compose an imaginary conversation in which you interview a calliope.*

Dog Around the Block

Dog around the block, sniff,
Hydrant sniffing, corner, grating,
Sniffing, always, starting forward,
Backward, dragging, sniffing backward,
Leash at taut, leash at dangle,
Leash in people's feet entangle —
Sniffing dog, apprised of smellings,
Meeting enemies,
Loving old acquaintances, sniff,
Sniffing hydrant for reminders,
Leg against the wall, raise,
Leaving grating, corner greeting,
Chance for meeting, sniff, meeting,
Meeting, telling, news of smelling,
Nose to tail, tail to nose,
Rigid, careful, pose,
Liking, partly liking, hating,
Then another hydrant, grating,
Leash at taut, leash at dangle,
Tangle, sniff, untangle,
Dog around the block, sniff.

E.B. White

Questions:
1. What sounds do you hear in this poem?
2. How many words end in "ing"? What does the repetition of this sound contribute to the poem?
3. Why is the poem all one sentence?
4. Why does the poem begin and end with the same line?

Activities:
1. Read the poem from bottom to top, starting with the beginning of the last line.
2. Imagine that you are a dog. Write a poem about walking your owner around the block.

The Devil in Texas

He scattered tarantulas over the roads,
Put thorns on the cactus and horns on the toads,
He sprinkled the sands with millions of ants
So the man who sits down must wear soles on his pants.
He lengthened the horns of the Texas steer,
And added an inch to the jack rabbit's ear;
He put mouths full of teeth in all of the lakes,
And under the rocks he put rattlesnakes.

He hung thorns and brambles on all of the trees,
He mixed up the dust with jiggers and fleas;
The rattlesnake bites you, the scorpion stings,
The mosquito delights you by buzzing his wings.
The heat in the summer's a hundred and ten,
Too hot for the Devil and too hot for men;
And all who remain in that climate soon bear
Cuts, bites, and stings, from their feet to their hair.

He quickened the buck of the bronco steed,
And poisoned the feet of the centipede;
The wild boar roams in the black chaparral;
It's a hell of a place that we've got for a hell.
He planted red pepper beside every brook;
The Mexicans use them in all that they cook.
Just dine with a Mexican, then you will shout,
'I've hell on the inside as well as the out!'

Unknown

Activities:
1. Re-read "*Johnnie Crack and Flossie Snail*" (p. 7). Compare the effects achieved by the use of rhyme, rhythm, and onomatopoeia in both poems.
2. Write a poem about the "Devil" in the region where you live.

The Daniel Jazz

Darius the Mede was a king and a wonder.
His eye was proud, and his voice was thunder.
He kept bad lions in a monstrous den.
He fed up the lions on Christian men.

Daniel was the chief hired man of the land.
He stirred up the jazz in the palace band.
He whitewashed the cellar. He shovelled in the coal.
And Daniel kept a-praying: — "Lord save my soul."
Daniel kept a-praying "Lord save my soul."
Daniel kept a-praying "Lord save my soul."

Daniel was the butler, swagger and swell.
He ran up stairs. He answered the bell.
And he would let in whoever came a-calling: —
Saints so holy, scamps so appalling.

"Old man Ahab leaves his card.
Elisha and the bears are a-waiting in the yard.
Here comes Pharaoh and his snakes a-calling.
Here comes Cain and his wife a-calling.
Shadrach, Meshach and Abednego for tea.
Here comes Jonah and the whale,
And the Sea!
Here comes St. Peter and his fishing pole.
Here come Judas and his silver a-calling.
Here comes old Beelzebub a-calling."
And Daniel kept a-praying: — "Lord save my soul."
Daniel kept a-praying: — "Lord save my soul."
Daniel kept a-praying: — "Lord save my soul."

His sweetheart and his mother were Christian and meek.
They washed and ironed for Darius every week.
One Thursday he met them at the door: —
Paid them as usual, but acted sore.

He said: — "Your Daniel is a dead little pigeon.
He's a good hard worker, but he talks religion."
And he showed them Daniel in the lions' cage.
Daniel standing quietly, the lions in a rage.
His good old mother cried: —
"Lord save him."
And Daniel's tender sweetheart cried: —
"Lord save him."

And she was a golden lily in the dew.
And she was as sweet as an apple on the tree
And she was as fine as a melon in the corn-field,
Gliding and lovely as a ship on the sea,
Gliding and lovely as a ship on the sea,
And she prayed to the Lord: —
"Send Gabriel. Send Gabriel."

King Darius said to the lions: —
"Bite Daniel. Bite Daniel.
Bite him. Bite him. Bite him!"
Thus roared the lions: —
"We want Daniel, Daniel, Daniel,
We want Daniel, Daniel, Daniel.
Grrrrrrrrrrrrrrrrrrrrrrrrr
Grrrrrrrrrrrrrrrrrrrrrrrrrr"

And Daniel did not frown,
Daniel did not cry.
He kept on looking at the sky.
And the Lord said to Gabriel: —
"Go chain the lions down,
Go chain the lions down,
Go chain the lions down."

And Gabriel chained the lions,
And Gabriel chained the lions,
And Gabriel chained the lions,
And Daniel got out of the den,
And Daniel got out of the den,
And Daniel got out of the den.
And Darius said: — "You're a Christian child,"
Darius said: — "You're a Christian child,"
Darius said: — "You're a Christian child,"
And gave him his job again,
And gave him his job again,
And gave him his job again.

Vachel Lindsay

Questions:
1. Why is the title of the poem appropriate?
2. How do you account for the obvious anachronisms in the poem?

Activities:
1. Prepare for a choral reading portraying each character in the poem. Be careful to accentuate the many changes in rhythm.
2. Imagine that you are a gospel singer. How would it affect your reading of the poem?
3. Try performing the poem with a jug band accompaniment.

Cicada's a sting
of sound
never found
on the ground
or on the wing
his noise tears
crossgrain on the dry
blue jay of the sky
like an electric razor that needs repairs

Unknown

Questions:
1. After your initial reading of the poem, read only the first, second, and last lines. How does this reading differ from your first reading?
2. What aspects of the cicada are revealed in lines 3 to 8?

The Shell

I.
And then I pressed the shell
Close to my ear,
And listened well.

And straightway, like a bell,
Came low and clear
The slow, sad murmur of far distant seas,

Whipped by an icy breeze
Upon a shore
Windswept and desolate.

It was a sunless strand that never bore
The footprint of a man,
Nor felt the weight

Since time began
Of any human quality or stir,
Save what the dreary winds and waves incur.

II.
And in the hush of waters was the sound
Of pebbles, rolling round;
Forever rolling, with a hollow sound:

And bubbling seaweeds, as the waters go,
Swish to and fro
Their long cold tentacles of slimy grey;

There was no day;
Nor ever came a night
Setting the stars alight

To wonder at the moon:
Was twilight only, and the frightened croon,
Smitten to whimpers, of the dreary wind .

And waves that journeyed blind...
And then I loosed my ear. — Oh, it was sweet
To hear a cart go jolting down the street!

James Stephens

Questions:
1. *What do you think happened before the poem began?*
2. *What does the poet hear in the shell?*
3. *Which words or phrases express the sounds of those things the poet hears?*
4. *Why was it "sweet / To hear a cart go jolting down the street!"*

Activity:
1. *Listen to the sounds in a seashell. Write a poem about what you hear, including some indication of your feelings about those sounds.*

The Rat's Dance

The rat is in the trap, it is in the trap,
And attacking heaven and earth with a mouthful of
                                        screeches like torn tin,
An effective gag.
When it stops screeching, it pants

And cannot think
"This has no face, it must be God" or

"No answer is also an answer."
Iron jaws, strong as the whole earth

Are stealing its backbone
For a crumpling of the Universe with screechings,

For supplanting every human brain inside its skull with a
                                        rat-body that knots and unknots,
A rat that goes on screeching,

Trying to uproot itself into each escaping screech,
But its long fangs bar that exit—

The incisors bared to the night spaces, threatening the
                                        constellations,

The glitterers in the black, to keep off,

Keep their distance,
While it works this out.

The rat understands suddenly. It bows and is still,
With a little beseeching of blood on its nose-end.

Ted Hughes

Questions:
1. What effect is achieved by the repetition in the first line?
2. What words suggest the noises made by the rat in the trap?
3. What emotions are associated with the word "screeching"?
4. What is the relationship between the words "screeching" and "beseeching"?

Activities:
1. List all the words or phrases in the poem that appeal to you because of their sound qualities.
2. Write a poem about the sounds of pain.

Splinter

The voice of the last cricket
across the first frost
is one kind of good-by.
It is so thin a splinter of singing.

Carl Sandburg

Activity:
1. *Compare this poem with the first poem in the unit (on page 3).*

2 SIMILE

"...the presence of things present"

At a mantis
I brandish my hand — like
a mantis.

Katō Shūson

Like a conclusion
it crouches on the ground —
a toad.

Tomizawa Kakio

Questions:
Answer the following as they apply to both poems:
1. *What two things are being compared?*
2. *What word signals the comparison?*
3. *How is the comparison appropriate?*
4. *How does the comparison in the second poem differ from the comparison in the first?*

Activity:
1. *Classify the comparisons as either concrete to concrete or concrete to abstract.*

Without warning

As a whirlwind
swoops on an oak
Love shakes my heart

Sappho

Questions:
1. What are the concrete and abstract elements of the comparison?
2. What word signals the comparison?

August

August.
The opposing
of peach and sugar,
and the sun inside the afternoon
like the stone in the fruit.

The ear of corn keeps
its laughter intact, yellow and firm.

August.
The little boys eat
brown bread and delicious moon.

Federico Garcia Lorca

Question:
1. *How is the comparison in lines 4 and 5 appropriate to the month of August?*

Sweet Like a Crow

for Hetti Corea, 8 years old

"The Sinhalese are beyond a doubt one of the least musical
people in the world. It would be quite impossible to have
less sense of pitch, line, or rhythm"
—PAUL BOWLES

Your voice sounds like a scorpion being pushed
through a glass tube
like someone has just trod on a peacock
like wind howling in a coconut
like a rusty bible, like someone pulling barbed wire
across a stone courtyard, like a pig drowning,
a vattacka being fried
a bone shaking hands
a frog singing at Carnegie Hall.
Like a crow swimming in milk,
like a nose being hit by a mango
like the crowd at the Royal-Thomian match,
a womb full of twins, a pariah dog
with a magpie in its mouth
like the midnight jet from Casablanca
like Air Pakistan curry,
a typewriter on fire, like a spirit in the gas
which cooks your dinner, like a hundred
pappadans being crunched, like someone
uselessly trying to light 3 Roses matches in a dark room,
the clicking sound of a reef when you put your head into the sea,
a dolphin reciting epic poetry to a sleepy audience,
the sound of a fan when someone throws brinjals at it,
like pineapples being sliced in the Pettah market
like betel juice hitting a butterfly in mid-air
like a whole village running naked onto the street
and tearing their sarongs, like an angry family
pushing a jeep out of the mud, like dirt on the needle,

like 8 sharks being carried on the back of a bicycle
like 3 old ladies locked in the lavatory
like the sound I heard when having an afternoon sleep
and someone walked through my room in ankle bracelets.

Michael Ondaatje

A simile is a figure of speech in which two things, alike in some
way, are imaginatively compared.

Activities:
1. Examine the vivid similes in this poem.
2. Discuss habits that people have which irritate you.
3. Write a poem about one of these annoying habits, following the
   model of "Sweet Like a Crow."

'Do not seek...'

Do not seek
for gentleness it comes
as gentle as the moon
floats
through the day
as gentle as these white
flowers on my palm
flickering
in a sunless
rain-near
breeze

Neil Oram

Questions:
1. *What is illogical about the similes presented in this poem?*
2. *Can the absence of logic affect the sense of a poem?*

Activity:
1. *Write a poem about gentleness.*

Ebb

I know what my heart is like
 Since your love died:
It is like a hollow ledge
Holding a little pool
 Left there by the tide,
 A little tepid pool,
Drying inward from the edge.

Edna St. Vincent Millay

Questions:
1. *Why did the poet create such a complex simile in this poem?*
2. *What does "ebb" mean? What is the opposite of "ebb"? How does your understanding of the action of tides contribute to your appreciation of the poem?*

The Lesson

'Your father's gone,' my bald headmaster said.
His shiny dome and brown tobacco jar
Splintered at once in tears. It wasn't grief.
I cried for knowledge which was bitterer
Than any grief. For there and then I knew
That grief has uses — that a father dead
Could bind the bully's fist a week or two;
And then I cried for shame, then for relief.

I was a month past ten when I learnt this:
I still remember how the noise was stilled
In school-assembly when my grief came in.
Some goldfish in a bowl quietly sculled
Around their shining prison on its shelf.
They were indifferent. All the other eyes
Were turned towards me. Somewhere in myself
Pride like a goldfish flashed a sudden fin.

Edward Lucie-Smith

Questions:
1. *Read this poem again, omitting the last complete sentence. How is the strength of the poem dependent upon the impact of the simile contained within the last line?*
2. *What is the significance of the title?*

Activity:
1. *Write a poem about a dramatic moment in your life. Make certain that your poem ends with a strong simile.*

The Other Morning

When I got up the other morning,
Jenny had thrown the window shutters wide open
to the blue horizon. She was wearing her new
rose-colored dress that glittered
like the emerald sea at daybreak. Her hair tumbled down
over her shoulders like a small
golden waterfall.
                              Dante was playing
his harmonica, and one would say his fingers
dripped with music and water into his
mother's soul. Helen also came
to the house in the afternoon and brought three flowerpots,
our roses for tomorrow. I wandered about, I looked,
I found the papers on my table sympathetic,
the idea of war improbable.
No sort of coffin could possibly fit into the universe.
Indeed, I wanted to write to the world:
If ever I talk to you about
such things, know this: I will refer to a coffin
filled with sun.

Nikiphóros Vrettákos

Questions:
1. a) *What similes are contained in the first seven lines of the poem?*
    b) *What other images of everyday life are presented?*
2. *How do these similes and images lead to the unique image in the
    last two lines?*

The Black Angel

Where are the people as beautiful as poems,
As calm as mirrors,
With their oceanic longings —
The idler whom reflection loved,
The woman with the iridescent brow?
For I would bring them flowers.

I think of that friend too much moved by music
Who turned to games
And made a game of boredom,
Of that one too much moved by faces
Who turned his face to the wall, and of that marvelous liar
Who turned at last to truth.

They are the past of what was always future.
They speak in tongues,
Silently, about nothing.
They are like old streetcars buried at sea,
In the wrong element, with no place to go. . . .
I will not meet *her* eye,

Although I shall, but here's a butterfly,
And a white flower,
And the moon rising on my nail.
This is the presence of things present,
Where flying woefully is like closing sweetly,
And there is nothing else.

Henri Coulette

Question:
1.   Where are the people "as beautiful as poems"? How do you know?

Activities:
1.   Make a list of all the people the poet considers "as beautiful as poems." For each person, quote the description that the poet gives, and expand this description in your own words.
2.   Write a poem about the people you consider to be "as beautiful as poems."

3 METAPHOR

"...a mountain of abundance"

The Flame

One
red
cardinal

first
shooting
flame
of
spring

Raymond Souster

Questions:
1. What do you see?
2. What things are being compared? How?

Activity:
1. Make a list of other aspects of nature which might be considered "flames of spring."

Searching on the wind,
   the hawk's cry...
      is the shape of its beak.

J.W. Hackett

Questions:
1. What things are being compared?
2. What word signals the comparison?
3. Insert the word "like" after the word "is." How does this alter the comparison?
4. Is the comparison in this poem concrete or abstract?

After a heated argument
I go out to the street
and become a motorcycle.

Kaneko Tōta

Question:
1. Why did the poet "become a motorcycle"?

Activities:
1. Write a poem following Tota's model:
   After a ____
   I go out to the street
   and become a ____.
2. Write your own three-line poem.

Who comes?
Is it the hound of death approaching?
Away!
Or I will harness you to my team.

Unknown Inuit

Questions:
1. *What is the setting, and how does it contribute to the poem?*
2. *Why is "the hound of death" an appropriate description?*
3. *How does the poet demonstrate that he is not afraid of death?*

Waves

Waves
bow
before
the shore

courtiers
to their king

and then
withdraw.

Unknown (from the Arabic)

Activities:

1. *Identify and explain the comparisons in this poem.*
2. *Think of a body of water with which you are familiar. Write a poem about it that uses comparisons.*

Siesta

A mosquito
motors in the room,

a taxi
in the ghost town.

Somewhere
saloon doors
creak in the wind.

Ted Milton

Question:
1. What information do the nouns in this poem convey? What information do the verbs add to the nouns? What do the adjectives add?

Activity:
1. Integrate all the information you gathered in Question 1 and write an account of what you see happening in the poem.

The Humped Ox

His lips move ceaselessly
But they neither swell nor wear out;
His teeth are two handsome rows of coral;
His horns form a circle
That never closes;
His eyes immense pearls that gleam in the night;
His hump is a mountain of abundance;
His tail strikes the air
But is only half a fly-whisk;
His body is a well-filled coffer
Held up by four withered stalks.

Flavien Ranaivo

A metaphor is a figure of speech that imaginatively identifies one thing with another.

Activities:

1. Make a drawing of an ox. Label the parts with metaphors from the poem. For example, do not write "teeth," write "handsome rows of coral."
2. For all of the parts of the ox not described by the poet, create your own metaphors.

The Old Repair Man

God is the Old Repair Man.
When we are junk in Nature's storehouse he takes us apart.
What is good he lays aside; he might use it some day.
What has decayed he buries in six feet of sod to nurture
    the weeds.
Those we leave behind moisten the sod with their tears;
But their eyes are blind as to where he has placed
    the good.
Some day the Old Repair Man
Will take the good from its secret place
And with his gentle, strong hands will mold
A more enduring work — a work that will defy Nature —
And we will laugh at the old days, the troubled days,
When we were but a crude piece of craftsmanship,
When we were but an experiment in Nature's laboratory. . . .
It is good we have the Old Repair Man.

Fenton Johnson

Questions:
1. *What are the features of this sustained metaphor?*
2. *Are the comparisons predominantly concrete or abstract? How do you account for this?*

Activity:
1. *Imagine you are an old repair man. Write a dialogue between yourself and a child who has brought in an item to be repaired.*

Fourteenth Birthday

The Enemy, who wears
Her mother's usual face
And confidential tone,
Has access; doubtless stares
Into her writing case
And listens on the phone.

Her fortress crumbles. Spies
Who call themselves her betters
Harry her night and day.
Herself's the single prize.
Likely they read her letters
And bear the tale away,

Or eavesdrop on her sleep
(Uncountered and unchidden)
To learn her dreams by heart.
There is no lock will keep
A secret rightly hidden
From their subversive art.

But till the end is sure,
Till on some open plain
They bring her to her knees,
She'll face them down — endure
In silence and disdain
Love's utmost treacheries.

Phyllis McGinley

Activities:
1. *List all the words from the poem that support the idea of the mother as "The Enemy."*
2. *Write a description of the relationship between a parent and a child.*
3. *Write a poem about "Love's utmost treacheries," using a sustained metaphor.*

The Catch

It darted across the pond
toward our sunset perch,
weaving in, up, and around
a spindle of air,
this delicate engine
fired by impulse and glitter,
swift darning-needle,
gossamer dragon,
less image than thought,
and the thought come alive.
Swoosh went the net
with a practiced hand.
"Da-da, may I look too?"
You may look, child,
all you want.
This prize belongs to no one.
But you will pay all
your life for the privilege,
all your life.

Stanley Kunitz

Questions:
1. *What is "the catch"?*
2. *What are the two principal metaphors and how are they developed?*
3. *How do you interpret the repetition in the last three lines?*

The Bird

The bird you captured is dead.
I told you it would die
but you would not learn
from my telling. You wanted
to cage a bird in your hands
and learn to fly.

Listen again.
You must not handle birds.
They cannot fly through your fingers.
You are not a nest
and a feather is
not made of blood and bone.

Only words
can fly for you like birds
on the wall of the sun.
A bird is a poem
that talks of the end of cages.

Patrick Lane

Questions:
1. How is a bird a poem?
2. How is a poem a bird?

Activity:
1. Write a poem in which you look at something familiar in a new
    way. Explain in your poem how your new perception differs from
    the old one.

4 PERSONIFICATION

"...thoughts between fingers of steel"

Hunger

I come among the peoples like a shadow.
I sit down by each man's side.

None sees me, but they look on one another,
And know that I am there.

My silence is like the silence of the tide
That buries the playground of children;

Like the deepening of frost in the slow night,
When birds are dead in the morning.

Armies trample, invade, destroy,
With guns roaring from earth and air.

Kings and chancellors give commands,
I give no command to any;

But I am listened to more than kings
And more than passionate orators.

I unswear words, and undo deeds.
Naked things know me.

I am the first and last to be felt of the living.
I am Hunger.

Laurence Binyon

Questions:
1. Who is the speaker?
2. Is the speaker masculine or feminine?

Activities:
1. Write a character study of the speaker.
2. Write a paragraph in which you describe hunger as you have
    experienced it.

Bride

Joy comes to us as a bride
The first rains burst into bloom
Nightingales strike up a dance in our neighborhood
Elegant water nymphs bring songs
Thoughts turn into gold
And gold all conversation
Poets and girls
Learn kisses by heart
Someone arrives at the festival out of breath
It is Time with his flute

George Sarandáris

Personification is a figure of speech in which something is given human form, character, or traits.

Questions:
1. What is personified in this poem?
2. Why does Joy come to us "as a bride"?
3. a) Why does Time arrive "out of breath"?
   b) Why does Time arrive "with his flute"?

Time, Give Me the Secret

Time, give me the secret
that makes you younger as
you grow older!

Day after day, your past
falls away, and your future looms ahead,
— and your present:
always the same as the instant
of the almond blossoming!

Time without footprints:
tell me how your soul
daily flows through your body!

Juan Ramón Jiménez

Questions:
1. What is the secret that Time possesses?
2. What is Time?

Activity:
1. Write a dialogue that takes place between you and Time.

November

He has hanged himself—the Sun.
　　He dangles
A scarecrow in thin air.

He is dead for love—the Sun,
　　He who in forest tangles
Wooed all things fair

That great lover—the Sun,
　　Now spangles
The wood with blood-stains.

He has hanged himself—the Sun.
　　How thin he dangles
In these gray rains!

F. W. Harvey

Questions:
1. *Why does the Sun hang himself?*
2. *To what is the Sun compared?*
3. *What is the difference between "He has hanged himself—the Sun" and "The sun hanged itself"?*

Activity:
1. *Write a poem in which you personify the month of your birth.*

Death of a Pair of Shoes

They're dying on me! They've lived
Faithfully, Christian
Servants honored
And happy helping

And pleasing their master,
A tired traveler
Ready to quit
For peace of soul and foot.

These soles know. They know
Step by step long rambles
And wet days, floundering
Among slop and cobbles.

Even the color drains
From the sad skins
Which, plain as they were, livened
Some forgotten festival.

All this announces a ruin
I don't grasp. The affliction
Of living corrodes honor.
They're running. Specters! Shoes!

Jorge Guillen

Question:
1. What can you learn about someone from that person's shoes?

Activity:
1. Write a composition about your favourite pair of shoes.

Permanently

One day the Nouns were clustered in the street.
An Adjective walked by, with her dark beauty.
The Nouns were struck, moved, changed.
The next day a Verb drove up, and created the Sentence.

Each Sentence says one thing—for example, "Although it
    was a dark rainy day when the Adjective walked by, I
    shall remember the pure and sweet expression on her face
    until the day I perish from the green, effective earth."
Or, "Will you please close the window, Andrew?"
Or, for example, "Thank you, the pink pot of flowers on
    the window sill has changed color recently to a light
    yellow, due to the heat from the boiler factory which
    exists nearby."

In the springtime the Sentences and the Nouns lay silently
    on the grass.
A lonely Conjunction here and there would call, "And!
    But!"
But the Adjective did not emerge.

As the adjective is lost in the sentence,
So I am lost in your eyes, ears, nose, and throat—
You have enchanted me with a single kiss
Which can never be undone
Until the destruction of language.

Kenneth Koch

Questions:
1. *What effect does the Adjective have upon the Nouns?*
2. *Why is the Adjective feminine?*
3. *What aspects of human nature are addressed in this poem?*
4. *What is the significance of the title?*

Activity:
1. *Choose a group of words that are related to one another, such as
   the days of the week or the names of planets. Write a composition
   describing a human relationship among the members of that
   group.*

Thistles

Against the rubber tongues of cows and the hoeing hands of men
Thistles spike the summer air
Or crackle open under a blue-black pressure.

Every one a revengeful burst
Of resurrection, a grasped fistful
Of splintered weapons and Icelandic frost thrust up

From the underground stain of a decayed Viking.
They are like pale hair and the gutturals of dialects.
Every one manages a plume of blood.

Then they grow grey, like men.
Mown down, it is a feud. Their sons appear,
Stiff with weapons, fighting back over the same ground.

Ted Hughes

Question:

1. What qualities of thistles are revealed through the poem's central comparison?

Activities:

1. Pick out the most important word in this poem. Show how the action of the poem depends upon the word you have chosen.
2. Write a poem in which you include one of the three major kinds of comparisons: simile, metaphor, and personification.

King Juke

The jukebox has a big square face,
A majestic face, softly glowing with red and green
and purple lights.

Have you got a face as bright as that?

BUT IT'S A PROVEN FACT, THAT A JUKEBOX HAS
NO EARS.

With its throat of brass, the jukebox eats live nickels
raw;
It can turn itself on or shut itself off;
It has no hangovers, knows no regrets, and it never
feels the need for sleep.
Can you do that?
What can you do that a jukebox can't, and do it ten
times better than you?

And it hammers at your nerves, and stabs you
through the heart, and beats upon your soul —
But can you do that to the box?

Its resourceful mind, filled with thoughts that range
from love to grief, from the gutter to the stars,
from pole to pole,
Can seize its thoughts between fingers of steel,
Begin them at the start and follow them through in
an orderly fashion at the very end.
Can you do that?
And what can you say that a jukebox can't, and say
it in a clearer, louder voice than yours?
What have you got, a jukebox hasn't got?

Well, a jukebox has no ears, they say.
The box, it is believed, cannot even hear itself.
IT SIMPLY HAS NO EARS AT ALL.

Kenneth Fearing

Questions:
1. What makes the jukebox "king"?
2. What kind of ruler is "King Juke"?
3. Why is it that a jukebox has no ears?
4. "What can you do that a jukebox can't...?"

5 IMAGERY

"...that not extinguished fire"

If you are squeamish

Don't prod the
beach rubble

Sappho

Activity:
1. *Don't be squeamish. Prod the beach rubble. What do you use to prod it? What do you see? What do you smell? What do you hear?*

With a crunching sound
the praying mantis devours
the face of a bee.

Yamaguchi Seishi

Activity:
1. Imagine that you are a praying mantis. In one or two paragraphs, describe eating the face of a bee. Include as many sensations as possible.

January

The fox drags its wounded belly
Over the snow, the crimson seeds
Of blood burst with a mild explosion,
Soft as excrement, bold as roses.

Over the snow that feels no pity,
Whose white hands can give no healing,
The fox drags its wounded belly.

R.S. Thomas

Activities:
For Groups
1. a) *List the three words in this poem that you find to be the most*
        forceful. Explain your choices.
    b) *Beside the words you have chosen in (a), list any word(s)*
        from the poem that form a contrast. Explain the contrasts.
2. *Write a brief account of the wounding of the fox from the point of*
    view of one of the following: (a) a hunter, (b) a crazed hound, (c) a
    skittish horse, (d) the fox's mate, or (e) the fox.

The Delicately Sloping Neck

The delicately sloping neck
of the head of wheat—
the grains are turning yellow in the sun
and the light wind, in which it shakes out
its lifted hair,
is polishing them.
The head nods as it dreams,
dreaming of the thresher's bed,
of the grindstone
that makes the flour,
dreaming of the risen dough
of the bread of life,
the bread kneaded by hand,
and dreaming of the hand that casts the seed.

Miguel de Unamuno

Questions:
1. How does personification develop the image of the head of wheat?
2. Of what does the head of wheat dream? Why?

Activity:
1. Imagine that you are a film-maker, and describe the sequence of shots you would use to film this scene.

Subway

I thought that if he could stoop
to pick out rubbish, each piece
placed in his bag — a tedious job
in front of crowds, all day
the trains at a steady roar,
the lighting dim, the air stagnant —
from bin to bin, searching
to the bottom for gum wrappers,
crumpled newspapers, torn sandwich
bags, cigarette stubs, particles
clinging to his fingers. All this
without a word, bending
at the foot of a steel pillar,
it was not too much for me
to be witness.

David Ignatow

Questions:
1. What is the man's occupation? Justify your answer with specific reference to the poem.
2. What mood is created by the images in the poem?
3. What is the narrator's attitude toward the man? Why?

Activities:
1. Write a monologue from the point of view of the man picking out rubbish.
2. Write a paragraph describing a scene in the subway.

A Fire-Truck

Right down the shocked street with a siren-blast
That sends all else skittering to the curb,
Redness, brass, ladders and hats hurl past,
    Blurring to sheer verb,

Shift at the corner into uproarious gear
And make it around the turn in a squall of traction,
The headlong bell maintaining sure and clear,
    Thought is degraded action!

Beautiful, heavy, unweary, loud, obvious thing!
I stand here purged of nuance, my mind a blank.
All I was brooding upon has taken wing,
    And I have you to thank.

As you howl beyond hearing I carry you into my mind,
Ladders and brass and all, there to admire
Your phoenix-red simplicity, enshrined
    In that not extinguished fire.

Richard Wilbur

Questions:
1. *What words describe the motion of the fire-truck? How do they do it?*
2. *Why does the poet say to the fire-truck: "I have you to thank."?*

Activity:
1. *Write a composition in which you imagine what it is like to ride on the back of a fire-truck.*

Manhole Covers

The beauty of manhole covers — what of that?
Like medals struck by a great savage khan,
Like Mayan calendar stones, unliftable, indecipherable,
Not like old electrum, chased and scored,
Mottoed and sculptured to a turn,
But notched and whelked and pocked and smashed
With the great company names:
Gentle Bethlehem, smiling United States.
This rustproof artifact of my street,
Long after roads are melted away, will lie
Sidewise in the graves of the iron-old world,
Bitten at the edges,
Strong with its cryptic American,
Its dated beauty.

Karl Shapiro

Question:
1. What is beautiful about manhole covers?

Child on Top of a Greenhouse

The wind billowing out the seat of my britches,
My feet crackling splinters of glass and dried putty,
The half-grown chrysanthemums staring up like
    accusers
Up through the streaked glass, flashing with sunlight,
A few white clouds all rushing eastward,
A line of elms plunging and tossing like horses,
And everyone, everyone pointing up and shouting!

Theodore Roethke

Questions:
1. How do the various images all focus on the child?
2. To what or to whom does "everyone, everyone" refer?
3. Why is everyone "pointing up and shouting!"?

Activity:
1. Write a dramatic poem in which you are the centre of attention.

Memory from Childhood

A chilly and overcast afternoon
in winter. The students
are studying. Steady boredom
of raindrops across the windowpanes.

It is time for class. In a poster
Cain is shown running
away, and Abel dead,
not far from a red spot.

The teacher, with a voice husky and hollow,
is thundering. He is an old man badly dressed,
withered and dried up,
who is holding a book in his hand.

And the whole children's choir
is singing its lesson:
one thousand times one hundred is one hundred thousand,
one thousand times one thousand is one million.

A chilly and overcast afternoon
in winter. The students
are studying. Steady boredom
of raindrops across the windowpanes.

Antonio Machado
(translated by Robert Bly)

Questions:
1. Do any of the images in this poem reflect your feelings about
   school? Which ones?
2. How do the images in the middle three stanzas develop from those
   in the first stanza?
3. Why are the first and last stanzas identical?

Activity:
1. Imagine that you are sixty years old. Write about a pleasant
   memory from your school years.

Drawing by Ronnie C., Grade One

For the sky, blue. But the six-year-
old searching his crayon-box, finds
no blue to match that sky
framed by the window — a see-through
    shine
over treetops, housetops. The wax colors
hold only dead light, not this water-
    flash
thinning to silver
at morning's far edge.
Gray won't do, either:
gray is for rain that you make with
dark slanting lines down-paper
                        Try orange!

— Draw a large corner circle for sun,
    egg-yolk solid,
with yellow strokes, leaping outward
like fire bloom — a brightness shouting
flower-shape wind-shape joy-shape!

The boy sighs, with leg-twisting bliss
    creating...

It is done. The stubby crayons
(all ten of them) are stuffed back
bumpily into their box.

Ruth Lechlitner

Questions:
1.   What problem does Ronnie C. face?
2.   How does he solve the problem?
3.   What is his response to having solved the problem?

Activity:
1.   Write a poem with a crayon of your favourite colour.

Dawn

An angel, robed in spotless white,
Bent down and kissed the sleeping Night.
Night woke to blush; the sprite was gone.
Men saw the blush and called it Dawn.

Paul Lawrence Dunbar

Standing by my bed

In gold sandals
Dawn that very
moment awoke me

Sappho

Moon fades into dawn...
an ivory moth settles
within the lily.

J. W. Hackett

Question:
1. Which of the three poems do you think best describes dawn? Give specific reasons for your choice.

Activity:
1. List the important times of your day. Write a series of short poems corresponding to these times.

Woman

In a wax
Catastrophe
A queen bee
Pregnant with honey
Is still

Tomorrow
A civilization
Of wings
In the sun

Cécile Cloutier

Activity:
For Groups
1. a) *Isolate and discuss each image.*
   b) *Interpret the images collectively. (Do not overlook the title.)*
   c) *Try to form an interpretation of the poem that satisfies everyone in your group. Account for your success or failure.*

Apocalypse

An angel
like winged sunlight
Drowned himself
In the sea
So night descended
Over existence.

Pierre Chatillon

Activities:
1. Carry out the same group activity as you did for "Woman" (opposite).
2. Decide whether the images in this poem are more or less complex than those in "Woman."

Because I Never Learned
(For my brother John)

Because I never learned how
to be gentle and the country
I lived in was hard with dead
animals and men, I didn't question
my father when he told me
to step on the kitten's head
after the bus had run over
its hind quarters.

Now, twenty years later,
I remember only:
the silence of the dying
when the fragile skull collapsed
under my hard bare heel,
the curved tongue in the dust
that would never cry again
and the small of my father's back
as he walked tall away.

Patrick Lane

Questions:
For Discussion
1. *Was the poet cruel or compassionate?*
2. *Do you agree or disagree with this statement: "The poet wants to be gentle but does not know how to be."?*
3. *What was the relationship between father and son?*
4. *Has twenty years made a difference in the poet's attitude toward the event he describes?*

Digging

To-day I think
Only with scents — scents dead leaves yield,
And bracken, and wild carrot's seed,
And the square mustard field;

Odours that rise
When the spade wounds the root of tree,
Rose, currant, raspberry, or goutweed,
Rhubarb or celery;

The smoke's smell, too,
Flowing from where a bonfire burns
The dead, the waste, the dangerous,
And all to sweetness turns.

It is enough
To smell, to crumble the dark earth,
While the robin sings over again
Sad songs of Autumn mirth.

Edward Thomas

Questions:
1. What do the words "scent," "odour," "smell," "stink," "fragrance," and "aroma" convey to you?
2. Why does the poet use the words he does to suggest the things he smells?
3. What does the poet mean when he says, "It is enough/To smell"?

Activity:
For Groups
1. Write a one-act play in which the five senses are the principal characters, but only four of them may remain in existence. For example:
   a) A dictator allows subjects only four senses.
   b) The five senses are shipwrecked and there is only room in the lifeboat for four.
   c) Four senses conspire to murder an egotistical fifth.
      Create a dialogue of conflict and argument among the five senses, and resolve the conflict without outside intervention.

Pain penetrates

Me drop
by drop

Sappho

Questions:
1. What is pain?
2. What kind of pain penetrates "drop by drop"?
3. How does pain feel? Describe pain without using a simile or a metaphor.

Activity:
1. Create a single image expressing pain that you have felt.

from The Burning of the Leaves

Now is the time for the burning of the leaves,
They go to the fire; the nostril pricks with smoke
Wandering slowly into a weeping mist.
Brittle and blotched, ragged and rotten sheaves!
A flame seizes the smouldering ruin and bites
On stubborn stalks that crackle as they resist.

The last hollyhock's fallen tower is dust;
All the spices of June are a bitter reek,
All the extravagant riches spent and mean.
All burns! The reddest rose is a ghost;
Sparks whirl up, to expire in the mist: the wild
Fingers of fire are making corruption clean.

Now is the time for stripping the spirit bare,
Time for the burning of days ended and done,
Idle solace of things that have gone before:
Rootless hopes and fruitless desire are there;
Let them go to the fire, with never a look behind.
The world that was ours is a world that is ours no more.

They will come again, the leaf and the flower, to arise
From squalor of rottenness into the old splendour,
And magical scents to a wondering memory bring;
The same glory, to shine upon different eyes.
Earth cares for her own ruins, naught for ours.
Nothing is certain, only the certain spring.

Laurence Binyon

Question:
1. How is the imagery in the first two stanzas developed in the last two stanzas?

Activity:
1. Write a poem about an event or activity that seems mundane but is charged with significance for you.

The Loving Dexterity

The flower
    fallen
she saw it

    where
it lay
    a pink petal

intact
    deftly
placed it

    on
its stem
    again

William Carlos Williams

Question:
1. *What inferences can you draw about the flower, the woman, and the act of replacing the petal?*

Nantucket

Flowers through the window
lavender and yellow

changed by white curtains —
Smell of cleanliness —

Sunshine of late afternoon —
On the glass tray

a glass pitcher, the tumbler
turned down, by which

a key is lying — And the
immaculate white bed

William Carlos Williams

Questions:
1. What is the poet's vantage point?
2. What features of the room impress the poet? Why?

Activity:
1. Describe entering a strange room that impresses you.

The Fish

I caught a tremendous fish
and held him beside the boat
half out of water, with my hook
fast in a corner of his mouth.
He didn't fight.
He hadn't fought at all.
He hung a grunting weight,
battered and venerable
and homely. Here and there
his brown skin hung in strips
like ancient wall-paper,
and its pattern of darker brown
was like wall-paper:
shapes like full-blown roses
stained and lost through age.
He was speckled with barnacles,
fine rosettes of lime,
and infested
with tiny white sea-lice,
and underneath two or three
rags of green weed hung down.
While his gills were breathing in
the terrible oxygen
—the frightening gills
fresh and crisp with blood,
that can cut so badly—
I thought of the coarse white flesh
packed in like feathers,
the big bones and the little bones,
the dramatic reds and blacks
of his shiny entrails,
and the pink swim-bladder
like a big peony.
I looked into his eyes
which were far larger than mine
but shallower, and yellowed,
the irises backed and packed
with tarnished tinfoil
seen through the lenses
of old scratched isinglass.
They shifted a little, but not
to return my stare.
—It was more like the tipping
of an object toward the light.

I admired his sullen face,
the mechanism of his jaw,
and then I saw
that from his lower lip
— if you could call it a lip —
grim, wet, and weapon-like,
hung five old pieces of fish-line,
or four and a wire leader
with the swivel still attached,
with all their five big hooks
grown firmly in his mouth.
A green line, frayed at the end
where he broke it, two heavier lines,
and a fine black thread
still crimped from the strain and snap
when it broke and he got away.
Like medals with their ribbons
frayed and wavering,
a five-haired beard of wisdom
trailing from his aching jaw.
I stared and stared
and victory filled up
the little rented boat,
from the pool of bilge
where oil had spread a rainbow
around the rusted engine
to the bailer rusted orange,
the sun-cracked thwarts,
the oarlocks on their strings,
the gunnels — until everything
was rainbow, rainbow, rainbow!
And I let the fish go.

Elizabeth Bishop

Questions:
1. How is the imagery in "The Fish" and "The Catfish" (on the next
   page) similar? How does it differ?
2. Which poem is more effective in its use of imagery? Why?

The Catfish

I spent afternoons like an old man's drowsy years,
fishing the creek water, as frothed and gold as lager,
catching river cats beyond the ironwood spears.
But with every catch, I hoped there was another, bigger.

And began to think there was a king of catfish there,
inert as a sack of coins in the bottom mud, wise
as he meditated in his dream-dark lair,
from a tarbucket head and two pale green eyes.

From a study of the specimens expiring on the bank,
I formed a picture of the mammoth one: grumpy, old,
heavy as a tub of cheese, uncleansed by water, rank.
He oared himself erect inside my mind and glowed.

His skin was twisted like a woman's hose upon his sides,
his mouth was tasseled like a lamp with ancient hooks;
now this embodied silence simply lasts beneath the tides
as remote from baits and lures as from the flight of ducks.

I've thought upon my monster beyond the range
of credulity; accepted him as if he really existed
and shook the abutments of my reason. Beyond change,
in a myth beyond begetting, this thing has lasted.

The real ones, I have found, are mortal in the mind
as in the world of hooks and worms and lethal boys.
The dreamed one lasts on where he's never been,
untroubled as a star by hooks and facts and other toys.

Jack Matthews

The War God's Horse Song

I am the Turquoise Woman's son.
On top of Belted Mountain
Beautiful horses—slim like a weasel!
My horse has a hoof like striped agate;
His fetlock is like a fine eagle plume;
His legs are quick like lightning.
My horse's body is like an eagle-plumed arrow;
My horse has a tail like a trailing black cloud.
I put flexible goods on my horse's back;
The little Holy Wind blows through his hair.

His mane is made of short rainbows.
My horse's ears are made of round corn.
My horse's eyes are made of big stars.
My horse's head is made of mixed waters
(From the holy waters—he never knows thirst).
My horse's teeth are made of white shell.
The long rainbow is in his mouth for a bridle,
    And with it I guide him.
When my horse neighs, different-colored horses follow.
When my horse neighs, different-colored sheep follow.
    I am wealthy, because of him.

Before me peaceful,
Behind me peaceful,
Under me peaceful,
Over me peaceful,
All around me peaceful—
Peaceful voice when he neighs.
I am Everlasting and Peaceful.
I stand for my horse.

Unknown Indian (Navajo)

Activities:
1. *Prepare for and deliver a dramatic reading of this poem.*
2. *Write a poem that describes what it is like to ride the War God's horse.*

6 DICTION

"...swift, slow; sweet, sour; adazzle, dim"

The stillness of dawn:
  crashing between the branches,
    a solitary leaf.

J. W. Hackett

Activities:
1. Read the poem aloud, then read it aloud again, eliminating the word "crashing." Explain the difference between the two readings.
2. Read aloud the words that contrast with the word "crashing."

By T'ing Yang Waterfall

A strange, beautiful girl
Bathes her white feet in the flowing water.
The white moon, in the midst of the clouds,
Is far away, beyond the reach of man.

Hsieh Ling Yuen

Questions:
1. What do you know about the girl? How do you know it?
2. Why is the word "white" repeated?

On Watching the Construction of a Skyscraper

Nothing sings from these orange trees,
Rindless steel as smooth as sapling skin,
Except a crane's brief wheeze
And all the muffled, clanking din
Of rivets nosing in like bees.

Burton Raffel

Questions:
1. What is the dominant image in this poem? How are the other images related to it?
2. What statement is the poet making about human beings' relationship with nature?

Activities:
1. List all the words in the poem that refer to natural objects. Then list all the words that refer to manufactured objects.
2. List ten manufactured goods whose names are taken from natural objects— "bulldozer," for example.

Paradise

I blesse thee, Lord, because I GROW
Among thy trees, which in a ROW
To thee both fruit and order OW.

What open force, or hidden CHARM
Can blast my fruit, or bring me HARM
While the inclosure is thine ARM?

Inclose me still for fear I START.
Be to me rather sharp and TART,
Than let me want thy hand & ART.

When thou dost greater judgements SPARE,
And with thy knife but prune and PARE,
Ev'n fruitfull trees more fruitfull ARE.

Such sharpness shows the sweetest FREND:
Such cuttings rather heal than REND:
And such beginnings touch their END.

George Herbert

Activities:
1. *Write a poem on the model of "Paradise," imitating its rhyme scheme and creating three-line stanzas.*
2. *Find a word that will create the longest series of end rhymes.*

A Life

Innocence?
In a sense.
In no sense!

Was that *it?*
Was *that* it?
Was that it?

That was it.

Howard Nemerov

Questions:
1. What is the association between the first line and the last line of the poem?
2. What is the significance of the title?

Activity:
1. Read the first stanza aloud several times, varying the emphasis as the poet does in the second stanza.

Mortality

Grass of levity,
Span in brevity,
Flowers' felicity,
Fire of misery,
Wind's stability,
Is mortality.

Unknown

Question:
1. Which word is inconsistent with the other words in the poem?
   Why is it inconsistent?

Activity:
1. Devise a poem in which you use a series of words similar to each
   other in structure.

Good and Clever

If all the good people were clever,
  And all clever people were good,
The world would be nicer than ever
  We thought that it possibly could.

But somehow 'tis seldom or never
  The two hit it off as they should,
The good are so harsh to the clever,
  The clever, so rude to the good!

So friends, let it be our endeavour
  To make each by each understood;
For few can be good, like the clever,
  Or clever, so well as the good.

Elizabeth Wordsworth

Question:
1. a) *What are the two most important words in this poem?*
    b) *How does the poet use these words to pose a problem?*
    c) *How does she use the same words to offer a solution to the problem?*

when god decided to invent
everything he took one
breath bigger than a circustent
and everything began

when man determined to destroy
himself he picked the was
of shall and finding only why
smashed it into because

e.e. cummings

Questions:
1. a) *What words in the first stanza contrast with words in the*
   second stanza?
   b) *What is the relationship between the words "was" and*
   "shall"?
   c) *What is the relationship between the words "why" and*
   "because"?
2. *What difference is there between the way "god" operates and the*
   way "man" operates, as stated in the poem?

Kid Stuff   December, 1942

The wise guys
tell me
that Christmas
is Kid Stuff...
Maybe they've got
something there—
Two thousand years ago
three wise guys
chased a star
across a continent
to bring
frankincense and myrrh
to a Kid
born in a manger
with an idea in his head...

And as the bombs
crash
all over the world
today

the real wise guys
know
that we've all
got to go chasing stars
again
in the hope
that we can get back
some of that
Kid Stuff
born two thousand years ago.

Frank Horne

Questions:
1. What does the poem reveal about the character and background of
    the speaker?
2. Who are "the wise guys," "three wise guys," and "the real wise
    guys"? Are they the same people?

Activity:
For Groups
1. Write a paraphrase of this poem using more conventional
    language. (Do not forget to include the title.) Read your group's
    version to the class. After all the versions have been heard, discuss
    the strengths and weaknesses of all of them, including the original.

Alligator on the Escalator

Through the revolving door
Of a department store
There slithered an alligator.

When he came to the escalator,
He stepped upon the track with great dexterity;
His tail draped over the railing,
And he clicked his teeth in glee:
    "Yo, I'm off on the escalator,
    Excited as I can be!
    It's a *moving* experience,
    As you can plainly see.
    On the moving stair I go anywhere,
    I rise to the top
    Past outerwear, innerwear,
    Dinnerwear, thinnerwear —
    Then down to the basement with bargains
        galore,
    Then back on the track to the top once more!
    Oh, I may ride the escalator
    Until closing time or later,
    So tell the telephone operator
    To call Mrs. Albert Q. Alligator
    And tell her to take a hot mud bath
    And not to wait up for me!"

Eve Merriam

Question:
1. *How has the poet had fun with the selection of words (diction) in this poem?*

Chain Saw at Dawn in Vermont in Time of Drouth

1.
Dawn and, distant, the steel-snarl and lyric
Of the chain saw in deep woods:
I wake. Was it
Trunk-scream, bough-rip and swish, then earth-thud?
No—only the saw's song, the saw
Sings: *now!* Sings:
Now, now, now, in the
Lash and blood-lust of an eternal present, the present
Murders the past, the nerve shrieks, the saw

Sings *now*, and I wake, rising
From that darkness of sleep which
Is the past, and is
The self. It is
Myself, and I know how,
Now far off,
New light gilds the spruce-tops.
The saw, for a moment, ceases, and under
Arm-pits of the blue-shirted sawyer sweat
Beads cold, and
In the obscene silence of the saw's cessation,
A crow, somewhere, calls.

The crow, in distance, calls with the crystalline beauty
Of the outraged heart.

Have I learned how to live?

Robert Penn Warren

Questions:
1. How does the poet's diction establish similarities between a human being and a machine?
2. What is the most notable difference between a person and a machine?

Activities:
1. Try to recall the first moment when you knew you were alive. Write a poem about that moment.
2. Write a description of the piece of equipment that terrifies you most.
3. Human beings have invented many different kinds of machinery. Write a short story in which you imagine what sort of human being a machine would invent.

Pied Beauty

Glory be to God for dappled things —
  For skies of couple-color as a brinded cow;
    For rose-moles all in stipple upon trout that swim;
Fresh-firecoal chestnut-falls; finches' wings;
  Landscape plotted and pieced — fold, fallow, and plough;
    And all trades, their gear and tackle and trim.

All things counter, original, spare, strange;
  Whatever is fickle, freckled (who knows how?)
    With swift, slow; sweet, sour; adazzle, dim;
He fathers-forth whose beauty is past change:
                                        Praise him.

Gerard Manley Hopkins

Questions:
1. What does "pied" mean? Which words in the poem correspond to the word "pied"?
2. How do the contrasts in the line, "With swift, slow; sweet, sour; adazzle, dim;" correspond to the title?
3. Why does the poet use hyphenated words?

God's Grandeur

The world is charged with the grandeur of God.
 It will flame out, like shining from shook foil;
 It gathers to a greatness, like the ooze of oil
Crushed. Why do men then now not reck his rod?
Generations have trod, have trod, have trod;
 And all is seared with trade; bleared, smeared with toil;
 And wears man's smudge and shares man's smell: the soil
Is bare now, nor can foot feel, being shod.

And for all this, nature is never spent;
 There lives the dearest freshness deep down things;
And though the last lights off the black West went
 Oh, morning, at the brown brink eastward, springs—
Because the Holy Ghost over the bent
 World broods with warm breast and with ah! bright wings.

Gerard Manley Hopkins

Question:
1. What does the word "charged" suggest to you?

Activity:
1. List all the words in the poem that "charge" the world. Categorize
    the words you have selected by part of speech. Which part of
    speech dominates? Why?

Quinnapoxet

I was fishing in the abandoned reservoir
back in Quinnapoxet,
where the snapping turtles cruised
and the bullheads swayed
in their bower of tree-stumps,
sleek as eels and pigeon-fat.
One of them gashed my thumb
with a flick of his razor fin
when I yanked the barb
out of his gullet.
The sun hung its terrible coals
over Buteau's farm: I saw
the treetops seething.

They came suddenly into view
on the Indian road,
evenly stepping
past the apple orchard,
commingling with the dust
they raised, their cloud of being,
against the dripping light
looming larger and bolder.
She was wearing a mourning bonnet
and a wrap of shining taffeta.
"Why don't you write?" she cried
from the folds of her veil.

"We never hear from you."
I had nothing to say to her.
But for him who walked behind her
in his dark worsted suit,
with his face averted
as if to hide a scald,
deep in his other life,
I touched my forehead
with my swollen thumb
and splayed my fingers out—

in deaf-mute country
the sign for father.

Stanley Kunitz

Questions:

1. What is the relationship between the first stanza and the rest of the
    poem?

For Discussion

2. What is a word?
3. How does a word convey meaning?

Activity:

1. Imagine that you are a deaf mute. Consider what words would
    mean to you. Choose the words from this poem that you think
    would be most difficult for you to understand.

7 SYNTAX

"without breaking anything"

Activities:
1. *Before reading the poem below, cover it up with a sheet of paper. Then rearrange the fourteen words in the following sentence to create as many new sentences as possible. Be sure to use all fourteen words, and be sure that your sentences make sense.*

   I have nothing to say and I am saying it and that is poetry.

Opening the Cage: 14 variations on 14 words

I have nothing to say and I am saying it and that is poetry. John Cage

I have to say poetry and is that nothing and am I saying it

I am and I have poetry to say and is that nothing saying it

I am nothing and I have poetry to say and that is saying it

I that am saying poetry have nothing and it is I and to say

And I say that I am to have poetry and saying it is nothing

I am poetry and nothing and saying it is to say that I have

To have nothing is poetry and I am saying that and I say it

Poetry is saying I have nothing and I am to say that and it

Saying nothing I am poetry and I have to say that and it is

It is and I am and I have poetry saying say that to nothing

It is saying poetry to nothing and I say I have and am that

Poetry is saying I have it and I am nothing and to say that

And that nothing is poetry I am saying and I have to say it

Saying poetry is nothing and to that I say I am and have it

Edwin Morgan

2. *Now that you've read the poem, compare your sentences with Edwin Morgan's. How many of his sentences make sense? How many of yours are different from his?*

With his venom

Irresistible
and bittersweet

that loosener
of limbs, Love

reptile-like
strikes me down

Sappho

Activities:
1. Rearrange the order of the lines to form a new poem that makes sense. Read your poem to the class.
2. Choose a short poem that you composed in a previous activity. Rearrange the lines to produce a more powerful, dramatic, or unusual effect.

Darting dragon-fly...
  Pull off its shiny wings and look...
Bright red pepper-pod.

Kikaku

Bright red pepper-pod...
  It needs but shiny wings and look...
Darting dragon-fly!

Basho

Activity:
1. Write two haiku that imitate what Kikaku and Basho have done.

The Base Stealer

Poised between going on and back, pulled
Both ways taut like a tightrope-walker,
Fingertips pointing the opposites,
Now bouncing tiptoe like a dropped ball
Or a kid skipping rope, come on, come on,
Running a scattering of steps sidewise,
How he teeters, skitters, tingles, teases,
Taunts them, hovers like an ecstatic bird,
He's only flirting, crowd him, crowd him,
Delicate, delicate, delicate, delicate — now!

Robert Francis

Syntax is a term that refers to the arrangement of words to form phrases, clauses, or sentences.

Questions:
1. How does the diction convey the tension of the base stealer?
2. How does the syntax convey tension?
3. Why is this poem all one sentence?

Activity:
1. Imagine that you are a runner about to steal a base. List all of the factors you must consider before making your move.

Come in kayaks
Help
My body stiffens.
All my limbs stiffen
My legs stiffen
My hands stiffen
I, I am becoming stone.

Unknown Inuit (Caribou)

Question:
1. How does the syntax lead the reader to the last line of the poem?

Activity:
1. Note the qualities of Inuit sculpture that are evident in the poem, and write a description of a piece of Inuit sculpture.

The dead who climb up to the sky
climb up steps
to the sky
up worn steps
all the dead who climb up to the sky
on worn steps
worn from the other side
worn from the inside
climb up to the sky

Unknown Inuit (Ammassalik)

Activities:
1. *a) List all the words in the poem that are repeated and indicate
        the number of times they are repeated.*
    b) Explain why each word is repeated each time it is repeated.
2. *Underline the words that you would emphasize in an oral reading,
    and then prepare and deliver a reading.*

Foul Shot

With two 60's stuck on the scoreboard
And two seconds hanging on the clock,
The solemn boy in the center of eyes,
Squeezed by silence,
Seeks out the line with his feet,
Soothes his hands along his uniform,
Gently drums the ball against the floor,
Then measures the waiting net,
Raises the ball on his right hand,
Balances it with his left,
Calms it with fingertips,
Breathes,
Crouches,
Waits,
And then through a stretching of stillness,
Nudges it upward.

The ball
Slides up and out,
Lands,
Leans,
Wobbles,
Wavers,
Hesitates,
Exasperates,
Plays it coy

Until every face begs with unsounding screams —

And then
            And then
                        And then,

Right before ROAR-UP,
Dives down and through.

Edwin A. Hoey

Activities:
1. *Compare the poet's syntax in describing the actions of the boy and the actions of the ball.*
2. *Compare Hoey's use of syntax with Francis' use of syntax in "The Base Stealer" on page 110.*

Eleven

And summer mornings, the mute child, rebellious,
Stupid, hating the words, the meanings, hating
The Think now, Think, the Oh but Think! would leave
On tiptoe the three chairs on the veranda
And crossing tree by tree the empty lawn
Push back the shed door and upon the sill
Stand pressing out the sunlight from his eyes
And enter and with outstretched fingers feel
The grindstone and behind it the bare wall
And turn and in the corner on the cool
Hard earth sit listening. And one by one,
Out of the dazzled shadow in the room,
The shapes would gather, the brown plowshare, spades,
Mattocks, the polished helves of picks, a scythe
Hung from the rafters, shovels, slender tines
Glinting across the curve of sickles — shapes
Older than men were, the wise tools, the iron
Friendly with earth. And sit there, quiet, breathing
The harsh dry smell of withered bulbs, the faint
Odor of dung, the silence. And outside
Beyond the half-shut door the blind leaves
And the corn moving. And at noon would come,
Up from the garden, his hard crooked hands
Gentle with earth, his knees still earth-stained, smelling
Of sun, of summer, the old gardener, like
A priest, like an interpreter, and bend
Over his baskets.
                    And they would not speak:
They would say nothing. And the child would sit there
Happy as though he had no name, as though
He had been no one: like a leaf, a stem,
Like a root growing —

Archibald MacLeish

Questions:

1. Why does the boy leave the veranda?
2. What is the attraction of the shed to the boy?
3. How is the gardener different from the boy's parents?

Activities:

1. a) Copy the poem into your notebook, omitting all punctuation.
   b) Read the poem silently, marking all the places where you pause.
   c) Listen carefully to several classmates' readings and compare the pauses others make with your own. How do the pauses affect the sense of the poem?
2. Write a poem or story about a place where you go when you are upset. Try to convey your reasons for going there.

Resolve

I must go back to the small place,
to the swept place,
to the still place,
to the silence under the drip of the dew,
under the beat of the bird's pulse,
under the whir of the gnat's wing,
to the silence under the absence of noise,
there bathe my hands and my heart
in the hush,
there rinse my ears and my eyes,
there know Thy voice and Thy face,
until when, O my God, do I knock
with motionless knuckles
on the crystal door of the air
hung on the hinge of the wind.

Vassar Miller

Question:
1. *Do you have a place like the poet's? How does your place differ from the poet's?*

Activity:
1. a) *Remove the prepositional phrases from the poem. What remains?*
   b) *Replace the prepositional phrases one by one. What does each successive phrase add to the poem?*

Spring is like a perhaps hand
(which comes carefully
out of Nowhere)arranging
a window,into which people look(while
people stare
arranging and changing placing
carefully there a strange
thing and a known thing here)and

changing everything carefully

spring is like a perhaps
Hand in a window
(carefully to
and fro moving New and
Old things,while
people stare carefully
moving a perhaps
fraction of flower here placing
an inch of air there)and

without breaking anything.

e.e. cummings

Questions:
1.   How and why does the poet use parentheses?
2.   How and why does the poet use capitalized words?

Activity:
1.   a)   Remove the word "perhaps."
     b)   Rewrite the first line, beginning with the word "perhaps."
     c)   Rewrite the first line, putting "perhaps" in five different places
          but leaving the other words in order. What do you notice about
          the progression?

The Universe

                    What
                    is it about,
                              the universe
                    about
us stretching out? We within our brains within it think
          we must unspin the laws that spin it. We think
                    why because
                                        we think

                    because.
                    Because
                                        we think
                                        we think

                              the universe
                    about
          us.
                    But does it think,
                    the universe?
          Then what
                    about?
                    About
us? If not, must there be cause
                    in the universe?
Must it have laws? And what
                    if the universe
          is *not about*
us? Then what?
                    What
                    is it about
                    and what
                    about
                         us?

                                        May Swenson

Activity:
1. *In order to facilitate the reading and understanding of this poem,
    rewrite it in your notebook. Do not change the order of the words,
    but rearrange them on the page in prose form. Suggest reasons
    why the poet has arranged the words as she has.*

If—

If you can keep your head when all about you
　　Are losing theirs and blaming it on you,
If you can trust yourself when all men doubt you,
　　But make allowance for their doubting too;
If you can wait and not be tired by waiting,
　　Or being lied about, don't deal in lies,
Or being hated, don't give way to hating,
　　And yet don't look too good, nor talk too wise:

If you can dream—and not make dreams your master;
　　If you can think—and not make thoughts your aim;
If you can meet with Triumph and Disaster
　　And treat those two impostors just the same;
If you can bear to hear the truth you've spoken
　　Twisted by knaves to make a trap for fools,
Or watch the things you gave your life to, broken,
　　And stoop and build 'em up with worn-out tools:

If you can make one heap of all your winnings
　　And risk it on one turn of pitch-and-toss,
And lose, and start again at your beginnings
　　And never breathe a word about your loss;
If you can force your heart and nerve and sinew
　　To serve your turn long after they are gone,
And so hold on when there is nothing in you
　　Except the Will which says to them: 'Hold on!'

If you can talk with crowds and keep your virtue,
　　Or walk with Kings—nor lose the common touch,
If neither foes nor loving friends can hurt you,
　　If all men count with you, but none too much;
If you can fill the unforgiving minute
　　With sixty seconds' worth of distance run,
Yours is the Earth and everything that's in it,
　　And—which is more—you'll be a Man, my son!

Rudyard Kipling

Questions:

For Discussion

1. In your opinion, what is the most important piece of advice this father gives to his son?
2. What is the effect of beginning so many lines with the word "if"?

Activities:

1. Re-read the poem, placing the last two lines first. Compare this version with the original.
2. Suggest reasons why the poem is all one sentence.

Model Parents

There are parents who punish their children.
Others who scold them
Bother them
Badger them
Lecture them
Sicken them
Break them in
Cut them off
Keep them under and
Pull their ears.

Others who reason with them
Jaw them
Worry them
Confine them, bore
Them to death, chide

Them, chivy
Them, crush
Them, curse
Them and disinherit them.

There are also parents who chastise them.
Parents who pinch them
Strike them
Slap them
Spank them
Torment them
Knock them around
Smash them to bits
Hand them over to the Social Welfare and then
Go to bed and make others.

Then there are the ones who
Take away their dessert, keep them
From sleeping, forbid
Them to go out, cut off
Their pocket money, tell them to
Shut up.

Finally, there are those who give them
A good swift kick in the pants and a
Father's blessing on New Year's Day.

Eloi de Grandmont

Activities:
1. Compare the syntax of this poem to the syntax of "If" (page 119). Show how the syntax in each poem is appropriate to its tone and content.
2. Write a composition about the characteristics you would expect to find in "model parents."

8 MOOD

"A rich dark suffering joy…"

Twilight Entered My Room

Twilight entered my room
like a red lion.
Its reflected light fell in the mirror
and I felt its soft paws
touching my naked feet.
I stooped under the table
which the day's work had blessed
and saw the sun kissing my feet
with its red tongue.

Pandelis Prevelakis

Questions:
1. What types of comparisons are used in this poem?
2. What mood is created through these devices?

Activity:
1. Write a composition in which you express the feelings you would experience if a lion were licking your feet.

True Enjoyment

I drink tea on the terrace at sunset all alone.
Spring breezes fan me as I moisten my brush on stone.
Sitting in perfect comfort, I write a poem on a palm.
A kingfisher chirps on a bamboo clothes-rack safe from harm;
A dragonfly clings to a fishing line, buzzing his warm refrain.
Now that I know what enjoyment is,
I'll come here again and again!

Unknown Chinese

Question:
1. *What actions and sensations persuade the poet to return to this place "again and again"?*

Activities:
1. *List three aspects of nature that arouse in you a feeling of contentment.*
2. *Based on this list, write a poem creating a single mood.*

Morning Mood

I wake with morning yawning in my mouth,
With laughter, see a teakettle spout steaming.
I wake with hunger in my belly
And I lie still, so beautiful it is, it leaves me dazed,
The timelessness of the light.

Grandma cares for me, and our family needs nothing more.
They share each other for pleasure
As mother knows, who learns of happiness
From her own actions
They did not even try to be beautiful, only true,
But beauty is here, it is a custom.

This place of unbroken joy,
Giving out its light today — only today — not tomorrow.

M. Panegoosho

Questions:
1. What images in the poem draw your attention the most? Why?
2. Which aspect of waking do you think is most important to the poet?

Activities:
1. Write a poem about the way in which you wake up in the morning.
2. Write a poem about the way you would like to wake up in the morning.
3. Make a tape recording of the conversation that takes place at your breakfast table one morning. Write it out as a dialogue.

The Weather

Live for myself
said the wind
Live for myself
said the rain
Live for myself
said the night
I bent my head
turned up my collar

David Ignatow

Questions:
1. Are the statements made by the wind, the rain, and the night imperative or assertive?
2. How do you account for the actions of the poet?

Activity:
1. Write a composition in which you express your thoughts and feelings as a pedestrian caught in a rainstorm.

'Now I Have Nothing'

Now I have nothing. Even the joy of loss —
Even the dreams I had I now am losing.
Only this thing I know; that you are using
My heart as a stone to bear your foot across....
I am glad — I am glad — the stone is of your choosing....

Stella Benson

Questions:
1. Do you accept the poet's opening statement?
2. How does the mood expressed in the last line differ from the mood expressed in the first? How do you account for this difference?

It's not me who goes singing...

It's not me who goes singing
   But the flowers I walk past
It's not me who goes laughing
   But the wine I still taste
It's not me who goes weeping
   But the love I have lost

Jacques Prévert

Questions:
1. What is the relationship between the first four lines and the last two?
2. What is the predominant mood that the poem creates in you?

empty room:
one swinging coat hanger
measures the silence

Jack Cain

Question:

1. How does diction convey mood in this poem?

Activity:

1. a) Write a paragraph in which you describe the circumstances
        leading to the event described in this poem. Does your
        paragraph convey the same mood as that of the poem?

    b) Compare the situation and mood presented in your paragraph
        with that of your classmates' paragraphs. Does the poem
        accommodate all of these moods?

Dew on the Young Garlic Leaves

The dew on the garlic
Is gone soon after sunrise.
The dew that evaporated this morning
Will descend again in tomorrow's dawn.
Man dies and is gone,
And when has anybody ever come back?

T'ien Hung

Questions:
1. What comparison is made in the poem?
2. What mood does the last line evoke?

To look at any thing

To look at any thing,
If you would know that thing,
You must look at it long:
To look at this green and say
"I have seen spring in these
Woods," will not do — you must
Be the thing you see:
You must be the dark snakes of
Stems and ferny plumes of leaves,
You must enter in
To the small silences between
The leaves,
You must take your time
And touch the very peace
They issue from.

John Moffitt

Activities:
1. a) Carefully list the instructions given by the poet.
    b) Identify the mood of each separate instruction.
    c) Describe the cumulative effect of these instructions.
2. Write out a list of instructions for someone to look at a thing worthy
    of contemplation.
3. Look at something. Be the thing you see. Write a poem about the
    experience.

To My Mother

Most near, most dear, most loved and most far,
Under the window where I often found her
Sitting as huge as Asia, seismic with laughter,
Gin and chicken helpless in her Irish hand,
Irresistible as Rabelais, but most tender for
The lame dogs and hurt birds that surround her, —
She is a procession no one can follow after
But be like a little dog following a brass band.

She will not glance up at the bomber, or condescend
To drop her gin and scuttle to a cellar,
But lean on the mahogany table like a mountain
Whom only faith can move, and so I send
O all my faith, and all my love to tell her
That she will move from mourning into morning.

George Barker

Questions:
1. *What aspects of the mother's character draw responses from her son?*
2. *What characteristics do you find most attractive about the woman?*
3. *What does the poet reveal about his own character?*

Activity:
1. *Write a poem which expresses your feelings about your mother.*

Girl with 'Cello

There had been no such music here until
A girl came in from falling dark and snow
To bring into this house her glowing 'cello
As if some silent, magic animal.

She sat, head bent, her long hair all a-spill
Over the breathing wood, and drew the bow.
There had been no such music here until
A girl came in from falling dark and snow.

And she drew out that sound so like a wail,
A rich dark suffering joy, as if to show
All that a wrist holds and that fingers know
When they caress a magic animal.
There had been no such music here until
A girl came in from falling dark and snow.

May Sarton

Activity:
1. a) *Listen to a recording of "The Swan" from Saint-Saens Carnival of the Animals.*
    b) *Record your impressions of the sound of the instrument. Are your impressions similar to those presented in the poem? Explain.*

Jamie

When Jamie was sixteen,
Suddenly he was deaf. There were no songs,
No voices any more.
He walked about stunned by the terrible silence.
Kicking a stick, rapping his knuckles on doors,
He felt a spell of silence all about him,
So loud it made a whirring in his ears.
People moved mouths without a sound escaping:
He shuddered at the straining of their throats.
And suddenly he watched them with suspicion.
Wondering if they were talking of his faults,
Were pitying him or seeing him with scorn.
He dived into their eyes and dragged up sneers,
And sauntering the streets, imagined laughter behind him.
Working at odd jobs, ploughing, picking potatoes,
Chopping trees in the lumber woods in winter,
He became accustomed to an aimless and lonely labour.
He was solitary and unloquacious as a stone.
And silence grew over him like moss on an old stump.
But sometimes, going to town,
He was sore with the hunger for company among the people
And, getting drunk, would shout at them for friendship,
Laughing aloud in the streets.
He returned to the woods,
And dreaming at night of a shining cowboy heaven
Where guns crashed through his deafness, awoke morose,
And chopped the necks of pine trees in his anger.

Elizabeth Brewster

Activities:

1. a) Carefully trace the sequence of Jamie's moods throughout the poem.

   b) For each mood you identify, list the words or phrases which express Jamie's feelings at that stage.

   c) Re-read the poem. Trace the sequence of your moods as you respond to Jamie's situation.

2. a) Imagine that you are deaf. List the things that you would miss most, in order of priority.

   b) Write an account of what it is to be deaf, directed to a person who can hear.

9 TONE

"...demons in the hedgerows"

Warning

When I am an old woman I shall wear purple
With a red hat which doesn't go, and doesn't suit me,
And I shall spend my pension on brandy and summer gloves
And satin sandals, and say we've no money for butter.
I shall sit down on the pavement when I'm tired
And gobble up samples in shops and press alarm bells
And run my stick along the public railings
And make up for the sobriety of my youth.
I shall go out in my slippers in the rain
And pick the flowers in other people's gardens
And learn to spit.

Jenny Joseph

Questions:
1. How old do you think the speaker is?
2. Why does she want to learn to spit?
3. What other actions described in the poem have something in common with learning to spit?
4. To whom is the poet issuing a "warning"?

Activities:
1. Read the poem aloud in the tone of voice you think is most appropriate.
2. Write a poem beginning with, "When I am old..."

Fatigue

I'm tired of Love: I'm still more tired of Rhyme.
But Money gives me pleasure all the time.

Hilaire Belloc

Activity:
1. *Read the poem aloud, using as many different tones of voice as you can.*

Thursday

And if I loved you Wednesday,
   Well, what is that to you?
I do not love you Thursday —
   So much is true.

And why you come complaining
   Is more than I can see.
I loved you Wednesday, — yes — but what
   Is that to me?

Edna St. Vincent Millay

Activity:
1.   *a)*   *Read this poem aloud in as flat a monotone as you can.*
     b)   *Read the poem aloud, exaggerating the intonation.*
     c)   *Compare the two readings. Then prepare for and deliver what you think is an appropriate reading.*

I hate and I love. And if you ask me how,
I do not know: I only feel it, and I'm torn in two.

Catullus

Activity:

1. *Devise a one-word title for this poem that is consistent with its tone.*

To a Fat Lady Seen From the Train

O why do you walk through the fields in gloves,
    Missing so much and so much?
O fat white woman whom nobody loves,
Why do you walk through the fields in gloves,
When the grass is soft as the breast of doves
    And shivering-sweet to the touch?
O why do you walk through the fields in gloves,
    Missing so much and so much.

Frances Cornford

Questions:
1. What situation is established by the title?
2. What concerns the poet most about the woman? Why is the poet so concerned?
3. How does the poet know that the woman is unloved?

Activities:
1. Read aloud only lines 1, 4, and 7. What tone is revealed in the reading of these lines?
2. Write a composition about someone you glimpsed while in transit.
3. Write a journal entry from the point of view of the woman.

If You Can Tell Me

if you
can tell me
why he left
I'll give you a shining ribbon
to tie
        or throw
                away
        just tell me.

a shining ribbon
        would look
                so pretty
in your hair.

I don't cry
        so don't worry
tell me,
        it would make me
        so happy
        to have the truth
                and
        to see a ribbon
        in your hair.

Sandra Abma

Questions:
1. *What is revealed in the first three lines?*
2. *Does the poet really want to be told the truth? Why or why not?*
3. *Which words or phrases are most indicative of the tone of this poem?*

Activities:
1. *Write a reply to the poet.*
2. *Write a composition in which you state an unusual reason for giving a gift to someone.*

I

My candle burns at both ends;
　It will not last the night;
But ah, my foes, and oh, my friends —
　It gives a lovely light!

II

Safe upon the solid rock the ugly houses stand:
Come and see my shining palace built upon the sand!

Edna St. Vincent Millay

Question:
1.　What is the relationship between these two poems?

I will walk with leg muscles
which are strong
as the sinews of the shins of the little caribou calf.

I will walk with leg muscles
which are strong
as the sinews of the shins of the little hare.

I will take care not to go toward the dark.
I will go toward the day.

Unknown Inuit (Iglulik)

Questions:
1. How is the tone developed through similes?
2. Is this tone changed in the last two lines?

Activities:
1. Write a composition in which you explain what the way people walk reveals about them.
2. List all the verbs you can think of to describe the way people walk. Explain the different meanings of the words you choose.

Ride a wild horse

Ride a wild horse
with purple wings
striped yellow and black
except his head
which must be red.

Ride a wild horse
against the sky
hold tight to his wings...
Before you die
whatever else you leave undone
once, ride a wild horse
into the sun.

Hannah Kahn

Questions:
1. *Where would you go if you could ride this horse?*
2. *What kind of sentence is used in this poem?*
3. *Why do you think the poet chooses to use sentences of this kind?*

Activity:
1. *Imagine that you are a stable owner. Write about the problems you would have in keeping a horse such as this.*

Deathwatch

All night long
thrown against
a buddy
slain
with his gnashing
teeth
bared to the full moon
with his bloated
hands
penetrating
my silence
I was writing
letters full of love

Never have I hugged
life
so hard

Giuseppe Ungaretti
(translated by Sonia Raiziss and Alfredo de Palchi)

Questions:
1. What is the poet contrasting in this poem?
2. What tone does the poet use?

To Satch

Sometimes I feel like I will never stop
Just go forever
Till one fine morning
I'll reach up and grab me a handful of stars
And swing out my long lean leg
And whip three hot strikes burning down the heavens
And look over at God and say
How about that!

Samuel Allen

Questions:
1. *How does the poet's diction convey his tone?*
2. *How do the metaphors support this tone?*

Activity:
1. *Describe an action, prompted by great joy, that you have taken or would like to take.*

Lament

Listen, children:
Your father is dead.
From his old coats
I'll make you little jackets;
I'll make you little trousers
From his old pants.
There'll be in his pockets
Things he used to put there,
Keys and pennies
Covered with tobacco;
Dan shall have the pennies
To save in his bank;
Anne shall have the keys
To make a pretty noise with.
Life must go on,
And the dead be forgotten;
Life must go on,
Though good men die;
Anne, eat your breakfast;
Dan, take your medicine;
Life must go on;
I forget just why.

Edna St. Vincent Millay

Question:
1. Is the word "lament" used in the title as a noun or as a verb? Which
   part of speech is more appropriate to the tone of the poem?

Activities:
1. Read the last sentence, omitting the last line. Now read the whole
   last sentence, noticing the difference in tone.
2. Write a composition explaining why life must go on.

Lies

Telling lies to the young is wrong.
Proving to them that lies are true is wrong.
Telling them that God's in his heaven
and all's well with the world is wrong.
The young know what you mean. The young are people.
Tell them the difficulties can't be counted,
and let them see not only what will be
but see with clarity these present times.
Say obstacles exist they must encounter
sorrow happens, hardship happens.
The hell with it. Who never knew
the price of happiness will not be happy.
Forgive no error you recognize,
it will repeat itself, increase,
and afterwards our pupils
will not forgive in us what we forgave.

Yevgeny Yevtushenko

Questions:
1. What do you notice about the sentences used throughout the poem?
2. If the poem were directed to a teacher, would you consider it good advice? Why?

Activity:
1. Write a letter to the editor of the school newspaper on the topic "Forgive no error," as it applies to education.

The Blue Dog
(for Gideon)

It used to work like this:
Teaching school I'd put
My feet up on the master's desk
Stare threatfully across the Daily Mirror
And say to them Today
I want a brown horse
In a green field. That way
They never bothered me.

But now I teach a boy
Who's always running out of paper
Wants fresh water finds fault with
His brush, paints a tractor driven
By his dad (puts trees/flowers/grass/the sky/the sun
Wrestles with demons in the hedgerows
Scatters flocks of birds
Runs screaming from the shadow in the righthand corner
                                        near his house
Whimpers and wipes his nose along his shirt
Cries Sir—cant manage it—the papers turning
Black.

I scold him—not unjustly—and
Help him with the horse
And show him green.
Today he comes to me and
Edges out his painting limp as rag.
The horse, I say, its blue—
The grass all black.
No Sir, he says, thats my dog,
I've got a blue dog.

Patrick Waites

Questions:
1. What is the teacher's attitude toward students, as revealed in the first stanza?
2. What does the boy do that annoys the teacher?
3. Is the teacher justified in scolding the boy?
4. Does the boy really have a blue dog?
5. Why does the tone change between the first stanza and the last?

Activity:
1. Write an account of an incident in which a teacher totally misconstrued your intentions.

Last Lesson of the Afternoon

When will the bell ring, and end this weariness?
How long have they tugged the leash, and strained apart,

My pack of unruly hounds! I cannot start
Them again on a quarry of knowledge they hate to hunt,
I can haul them and urge them no more.

No longer now can I endure the brunt
Of the books that lie out on the desks; a full threescore
Of several insults of blotted pages, and scrawl
Of slovenly work that they have offered me.
I am sick, and what on earth is the good of it all?
What good to them or me, I cannot see!

So, shall I take
My last dear fuel of life to heap on my soul
And kindle my will to a flame that shall consume
Their dross of indifference; and take the toll
Of their insults in punishment? —I will not! —

I will not waste my soul and my strength for this.
What do I care for all that they do amiss!
What is the point of this teaching of mine, and of this
Learning of theirs? It all goes down the same abyss.

What does it matter to me, if they can write
A description of a dog, or if they can't?
What is the point? To us both, it is all my aunt!
And yet I'm supposed to care, with all my might.

I do not, and will not; they won't and they don't; and that's all!
I shall keep my strength for myself; they can keep theirs as well.
Why should we beat our heads against the wall
Of each other? I shall sit and wait for the bell.

D.H. Lawrence

Questions:
1. *What is a teacher's responsibility to his or her students?*
2. *Does a teacher have the right to feel and act as this one does?*
3. a) *How is the tone of the first line developed in the sustained metaphor that follows it?*
   b) *How does the tone change in the second stanza?*
4. a) *What is the teacher's attitude toward his students in the last four stanzas?*
   b) *What is the teacher's attitude in the last two lines?*

Old Woman Seated

I am not to go into the attic
Because I am known to fall,
But when they are out
And the house cracks its joints
I am often there;
Wearing clothes which have been sent
To a jumble sale for Christian Aid,
Taking tea in a chair they do not like.

Sometimes I air decided views on
                                        the young,

Or read Mrs Henry Wood,
Or put some flowers in a clear vase
With the stem showing — which is
                                        not permitted.

When they return to find me a little tired
From not unravelling a sweater for Oxfam,
Or writing to a grandchild who will
                                        not reply,

They discuss me in voices that have had
The benefits of Speech Training,
And although dissatisfied —
They can't prove anything.

                                        Frances Gill

Questions:
1. Do you like this old woman? Why or why not?
2. Could this woman be the same one as in the poem "Warning" (page 141)?

Activity:
1. Sit down and have a conversation with the oldest person you know. You might wish to read this poem or "Warning" to that person. Discuss the experience with your classmates.

10 IRONY

"...how to avoid the obvious"

Maybe this road
leads nowhere but someone
is coming from there

Lars Norén

(translated by Gunnar Harding and W.S. Merwin)

Activities:

1. a) *Divide the poem into two logical parts. What expectation is established in the first part?*

    b) *What is the relationship between the second part and the first?*

2. *Following Norén's model, write a poem that tries to achieve a similar effect:*

    Maybe _____

    but _____

The Hunter

The hunter crouches in his blind
'Neath camouflage of every kind,
And conjures up a quacking noise
To lend allure to his decoys.
This grown-up man, with pluck and luck,
Is hoping to outwit a duck.

Ogden Nash

Question:
1. What expectation is established in the first sentence of the poem?

Activities:
1. Replace the word "outwit" with the word "shoot." How does this change affect the poem? Explain why the word "outwit" is critical to the poem.
2. Write a composition about the time, money, and energy people are willing to spend to catch a trout or shoot a deer.
3. Imagine that you are a duck flying over the hunter. Write a passage in which you reveal your thoughts and impressions of the hunter.

Surgeons Must be Very Careful

Surgeons must be very careful
When they take the knife.
Underneath their fine incisions
Stirs the culprit, life.

Emily Dickinson

Questions:
1. What is unexpected about the last line?
2. In what sense is life a "culprit"?

Birth

Perfect from the start
That small cell
Contains
Already
The wrinkles and death
Of an old man

Cécile Cloutier

Irony is a device in which the literal meaning of a word or statement is the opposite of that intended.

Question:

1. What is ironic about the title?

On the Birth of his Son

Families, when a child is born,
Want it to be intelligent.
I through intelligence,
Having wrecked my whole life,
Only hope the baby will prove
Ignorant and stupid.
Then he will crown a tranquil life
By becoming a Cabinet Minister.

Su Tung-P'o
(translated by Arthur Waley)

Questions:
For Discussion
1. How can you wreck your "whole life" through intelligence?
2. How can being "ignorant and stupid" give you a "tranquil life"?
3. What is the difference between ignorance and stupidity?
4. What does the poet imply about Cabinet Ministers? (Is he right?)

The Sky

The child looks upwards
At the blue sky above.
He lifts his tiny hand
And longs to touch the sky.

Unable to perceive
That the sky is an illusion:
The child thinks that he cannot reach it,
When he holds it in his hand.

Manuel Bandeira
(translated by Giovanni Ponteiro)

Questions:
1. Is the sky an illusion?
2. Is the child ignorant or innocent?
3. What does the child hold in his hand?

Activities:
1. Write a poem entitled "Illusions."
2. Write a composition about one of your childhood illusions that has been shattered.

Boy at the Window

Seeing the snowman standing all alone
In dusk and cold is more than he can bear.
The small boy weeps to hear the wind prepare
A night of gnashings and enormous moan.
His tearful sight can hardly reach to where
The pale-faced figure with bitumen eyes
Returns him such a god-forsaken stare
As outcast Adam gave to Paradise.

The man of snow is, nonetheless, content,
Having no wish to go inside and die.
Still, he is moved to see the youngster cry.
Though frozen water is his element,
He melts enough to drop from one soft eye
A trickle of the purest rain, a tear
For the child at the bright pane surrounded by
Such warmth, such light, such love,
    and so much fear.

Richard Wilbur

Questions:
1. *Why does the boy weep?*
2. *Why is the snowman content at first? Why does he weep later?*
3. *What causes the boy to be surrounded by fear?*

Activities:
1. *Write a poem about your fears.*
2. *Write a composition explaining why children build snowmen rather than other creatures.*

A Helping Hand

We gave a helping hand to grass —
    and it turned into corn.
We gave a helping hand to fire
    and it turned into a rocket.
Hesitatingly,
cautiously,
we give a helping hand
to people,
to some people...

Miroslav Holub

Questions:
1. *Why do people come last in the progression of the poem?*
2. *Why does the poet use two different tenses of the verb "to give"?*
3. *How do the adverbs in the poem contribute to the irony of the last line?*
4. *Why does the poem end in ellipsis points?*

Activity:
1. *Write a narrative that tells what happened the last time you gave someone "a helping hand."*

Summer Camp

Here is a lovely little camp
Built among the Laurentian hills
By a Children's Welfare Society,
Which is entirely supported by voluntary contributions.
All summer long underprivileged children scamper about
And it is astonishing how soon they look happy and well.
Two weeks here in the sun and air
Through the charity of our wealthy citizens
Will be a wonderful help to the little tots
When they return for a winter in the slums.

F.R. Scott

Activity:
1. *Prepare and deliver a reading of this poem as though you were a television commentator presenting a documentary on underprivileged children at a summer camp. Give careful attention to the poet's diction.*

Plucking the Rushes

A boy and girl are sent to gather rushes for thatching.
(Fourth or Fifth Century)

Green rushes with red shoots,
Long leaves bending to the wind —
You and I in the same boat
Plucking rushes at the Five Lakes.
We started at dawn from the orchid-island;
We rested under the elms till noon.
You and I plucking rushes
Had not plucked a handful when night came!

Unknown Chinese
(translated by Arthur Waley)

Questions:
1. *How is the last sentence in this poem ironic?*
2. *How does the irony differ from that in "Summer Camp" (page 169)?*

The Adversary

A mother's hardest to forgive.
Life is the fruit she longs to hand you,
Ripe on a plate. And while you live,
Relentlessly she understands you.

Phyllis McGinley

Questions:
1. For what is a mother to be forgiven?
2. What is the relationship between the title and the last line?

Follower

My father worked with a horse-plough,
His shoulders globed like a full sail strung
Between the shafts and the furrow.
The horses strained at his clicking tongue.

An expert. He would set the wing
And fit the bright steel-pointed sock.
The sod rolled over without breaking.
At the headrig, with a single pluck

Of reins, the sweating team turned round
And back into the land. His eye
Narrowed and angled at the ground,
Mapping the furrow exactly.

I stumbled in his hob-nailed wake,
Fell sometimes on the polished sod;
Sometimes he rode me on his back
Dipping and rising to his plod.

I wanted to grow up and plough,
To close one eye, stiffen my arm.
All I ever did was follow
In his broad shadow round the farm.

I was a nuisance, tripping, falling,
Yapping always. But today
It is my father who keeps stumbling
Behind me, and will not go away.

Seamus Heaney

Activities:
1. *Divide the poem into sections according to each change in focus. Explain what each section reveals about the poet's relationship with his father.*
2. *Is your father ever a nuisance? Compose a dialogue between you and your father in which you try to explain to him that he is a nuisance.*
3. *Narrate a specific incident from your childhood in which you "helped" your father with a task.*

Epitaph on a Tyrant

Perfection, of a kind, was what he was after,
And the poetry he invented was easy to understand;
He knew human folly like the back of his hand,
And was greatly interested in armies and fleets;
When he laughed, respectable senators burst with laughter,
And when he cried the little children died in the streets.

W.H. Auden

Questions:
1. What is an epitaph?
2. What is a tyrant?
3. Is this poem a suitable epitaph for a tyrant? Why or why not?

Activities:
1. Research the life of a tyrant and write a brief biography. You might wish to consider: Alexander the Great, Caligula, Hitler, Herod, Kubla Khan, Diocletian, Louis XIV, or Ivan the Terrible.
2. Write an epitaph for the tyrant you have chosen.

Whelk

The mollusc living in its shell
never found very much to say
to man
but dead it tells the ocean's tale
to ears of children listening
in hushed surprise
in hushed surprise

Raymond Queneau

Question:
1. What is achieved by the repetition at the end of the poem?

Activity:
1. Using only the poem for reference, explain what you think a
    "whelk" and a "mollusc" are. Use a dictionary to verify your
    definitions.

By Way of Error

Man
Has turned sails
One
By
One
And read
The big blue page
Of the sea

Then
He has built up
Some thousands
Of millions
Of miles
Of light cables

And he has given them
Some millions
Of thousands
Of knots

All to tie up the sea

Cécile Cloutier

Question:
1. Is the relationship between people and nature ironic as revealed in this poem?

Activity:
For Groups
1. Discuss the ironic relationship between people and nature, considering (a) road construction, (b) air conditioning, (c) owning real estate, (d) dams, (e) the Alaska pipeline, and (f) pesticides.

Pitcher

His art is eccentricity, his aim
How not to hit the mark he seems to aim at,

His passion how to avoid the obvious,
His technique how to vary the avoidance.

The others throw to be comprehended. He
Throws to be a moment misunderstood.

Yet not too much. Not errant, arrant, wild,
But every seeming aberration willed.

Not to, yet still, still to communicate
Making the batter understand too late.

Robert Francis

Questions:
1. How does the word "eccentricity" apply to the pitcher's aim?
2. What does the pitcher want to communicate to the batter?
3. What does the batter understand too late?

Activities:
1. List all the words and phrases you can think of that are peculiar to baseball—for example, "bull-pen," "dug-out."
2. Write a composition about an incident in which you "let the team down."

Don Larsen's Perfect Game

Everybody went to bat three times
except their pitcher (twice) and his pinch hitter,
but nobody got anything at all.
Don Larsen in the eighth and ninth looked pale
and afterwards he did not want to talk.
This is a fellow who will have bad dreams.
His catcher Berra jumped for joy and hugged him
like a bear, legs and arms, and all the Yankees
crowded around him thick to make him be
not lonely, and in fact in fact in fact
nothing went wrong. But that was yesterday.

Paul Goodman

Questions:
1. *Why does Don Larsen look pale "in the eighth and ninth"?*
2. *Why will he have bad dreams?*
For Discussion
3. a) *What is perfection?*
   b) *What is wrong with perfection?*

Activities:
1. *Write a composition about a person, thing, or event which you consider to be perfect.*
2. *Write a poem about a personal triumph.*

Modern Ode to the Modern School

Just after the Board had brought the schools up to date
To prepare you for your Life Work
Without teaching you one superfluous thing,
Jim Reilly presented himself to be educated.
He wanted to be a bricklayer.
They taught him to be a perfect bricklayer.
And nothing more.

He knew so much about bricklaying
That the contractor made him a foreman
But he knew nothing about being a foreman.
He spoke to the School Board about it,
And they put in a night course
On how to be a foreman
And nothing more.

He became so excellent a foreman
That the contractor made him a partner.
But he knew nothing about figuring costs
Nor about bookkeeping
Nor about real estate,
And he was too proud to go back to night school.
So he hired a tutor
Who taught him these things
And nothing more.

Prospering at last
And meeting other men as prosperous,
Whenever the conversation started, he'd say to himself
"Just wait till it comes my way—
Then I'll show them!"
But they never mentioned bricklaying
Nor the art of being a foreman
Nor the whole duty of contractors,
Nor even real estate.
So Jim never said anything.

John Erskine

Activity:
1. Write a composition about the ironies of your own education. Send a copy to the director of your local board of education.

11 FORM

"the image
the transformation"

She Loves Me

Emmett Williams

Questions:
1. What does the poem's form represent?
2. How does the content differ from the content of traditional poems?

Activity:
1. Write a composition explaining why people give flowers to others whom they love.

Football Forms

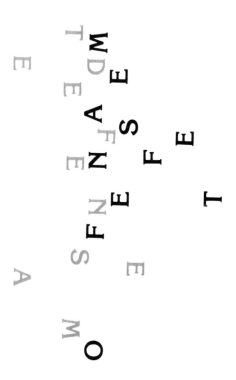

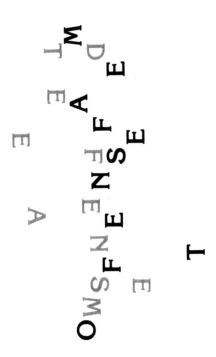

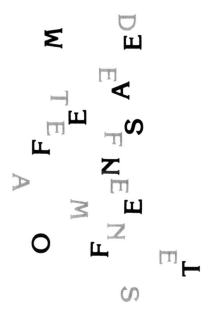

Richard Kostelanetz

Activities:
1. Discuss with a football player or fan whether this is a passing play or a running play.
2. Devise your own play with the same teams.

Ice Cream

```
                    ice cream
                    i scream
                    ice cream
        bright
        chosen                                blurred
        lucent                                rounded off
        sharp                                 made indefinite
                                              The side
        uneven                                nubbled
        curving             the image         syrup-slow
        but willed          the transformation    the taste
        jagged                                glyceride
                            eating it         the memory
silent                                        smirched
magical, one                                  shimmering
moment only                                   insatiable

   melting                                       accumulating,
                                                 dribbling, about
        the shape itself                         the cone     to drop
        the texture                              cardboard
        a test                                   the surface
        an admission                       sticky as plastic

           the recognition         Immediate and
           deceiving the mind       unknown
           the lettering on the rim   trivial
           arguing sugar crystals   enormous
           blatant, gummy, broken
                                      licked
           the patchwork grill       moist
           intensifying              still
           curving                   firm

              outline                yet
              curling its            dis-
              fingers            appear-
              around,                ing
              and down

           possessing

           to draw, to take
           in  the  hand,
           to     crunch
             its     one
              point
```

Jonathan Price

Questions:

1. How is "the shape itself" related to "the image/the transformation" of the poem?
2. Why are there no complete sentences in the poem?

Activity:

1. Write a concrete poem about your favourite food.

Silence

silencio silencio silencio

silencio silencio silencio

silencio   silencio

silencio silencio silencio

silencio silencio silencio

Eugen Gomringer

Question:
1. What does the shape of this poem suggest about the nature of silence?

Activity:
1. Devise a concrete poem that expresses the way in which you experience silence.

collision

The sun
        threading
   through the

                        Spring-fresh
                      leaves

makes a
    dappled
  shifting
    pattern

          on the sidewalk

                  until it rams into
                  the hulking bulk
                  of the warehouse.

Harry Chapin

Question:
1. *What is the relationship between the form of this poem and the content?*

Lilac

Mary Ellen Solt

Question:

1. What do you find interesting and appealing about this poem?

Activity:

1. Make a pictorial design out of the letters of a word.

Point Scored

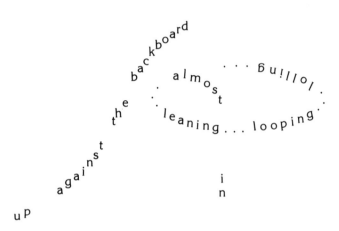

C. Cardenas Dwyer

Activity:
1. a) Compare this poem with "Foul Shot" (page 113) in form and
       content.
    b) Decide which poem makes more effective use of diction, and
       explain your reasoning.

Sweethearts

```
s  w  e  e  t  h  e  a  r  t  s
s  w  e  e  t  h  e  a  r  t  s
s  w  e  e  t  h  e  a  r  t  s
s  w  e  e  t  h  e  a  r  t  s
s  w  e  e  t  h  e  a  r  t  s
s  w  e  e  t  h  e  a  r  t  s
s  w  e  e  t  h  e  a  r  t  s
s  w  e  e  t  h  e  a  r  t  s
s  w  e  e  t  h  e  a  r  t  s
s  w  e  e  t  h  e  a  r  t  s
s  w  e  e  t  h  e  a  r  t  s
```

```
            t  h  e
s     e              a
s     e  e  t  h  e           s
```

```
            t  h  e
s  w  e  e  t  h  e  a  r  t  s
s     e  e  t  h  e
                     a        s
            t  h  e
s     e              a
s     e  e  t  h  e           s
```

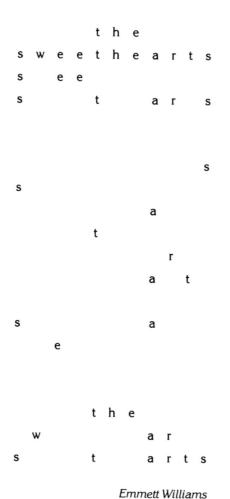

Emmett Williams

Question:

1. What is the relationship between "sweethearts" and the sea? And the stars?

Activities:

1. Arrange the word "sweethearts" in a new way, following the author's model.
2. Choose your own word and write a poem in this manner.

400-Meter Freestyle

THE GUN full swing the swimmer catapults and
    cracks
                                              s
                                              i
                                            x
feet away onto that perfect glass he catches at
a
n
d
throws behind him scoop after scoop cunningly
    moving
                                          t
                                          h
                                        e
water back to move him forward. Thrift is his
    wonderful
s
e
c
ret; he has schooled out all extravagance. No muscle
                                    r
                                    i
                                  p
ples without compensation wrist cock to heel snap to
h
i
s
mobile mouth that siphons in the air that nurtures
                                h
                                 i
                                m
at half an inch above sea level so to speak.

```
T
h
    e
    astonishing  whites  of  the  soles  of  his  feet  rise
                                              a
                                                n
                                                d
    salute us on the turns. He flips, converts, and is gone
    a
l
    l
    in one. We watch him for signs. His arms are steady
        at
                                            t
                                              h
                                                e
    catch, his cadent feet tick in the stretch, they know
    t
h
    e
    lesson well. Lungs know, too: he does not list for
                                            a
                                              i
                                                r
    he  drives  along  on  little  sips  carefully  expended
    b
u
    t
    that plum red heart pumps hard cries hurt how soon
                                            i
                                              t
                                                s
    near one more and makes its final surge
                        TIME: 4:25:9


                        Maxine W. Kumin
```

Questions:
1. What problems does this poem cause for the reader?
2. How successful is the form chosen by the poet?

Activity:
1. Write a concrete poem about a track and field event.

The Secret Sits

We dance round in a ring and suppose,
But the Secret sits in the middle and knows.

Robert Frost

Questions:
1. What is the relationship between the first and second lines in each epigram?
2. What is the tone of these two epigrams?

Activities:
1. Re-read the poems "Fatigue" (page 142), "I hate and I love" (page 144), and "Safe upon..." (page 147). Explain why these poems are successful epigrams.
2. Write several ironic epigrams of your own.

Forgive, O Lord

Forgive, O Lord, my little jokes on Thee
And I'll forgive Thy great big one on me.

Robert Frost

Sonnet 210

You seek the best that Nature can confer
Upon our universe? Then come and see
That beauty shining like a sun on me
And on the world, virtue's disparager.
Only, come soon; Death ever is astir
To seize the best, leaving the wicked free.
She is too lovely for mortality;
The gods are looking eagerly on her.
Come soon, and you will see all comeliness,
All virtue, and all gentle-mannered ways
Sweetly conjoined past any power to sever;
And you will vow my rimes are valueless,
You'll stand so dazzled in delicious maze.
— But if you linger, you will weep forever.

Petrarch

The following questions and activity refer to both sonnets.

Questions:
1. *To whom is the poet speaking?*
2. *Does the question asked by the poet require an answer? Why or why not?*
3. a) *How do the last two lines provide an appropriate conclusion to the poem?*
   b) *How are the endings of the two poems similar? How do they differ?*

Sonnet 18

Shall I compare thee to a summer's day?
Thou art more lovely and more temperate.
Rough winds do shake the darling buds of May,
And summer's lease hath all too short a date.
Sometime too hot the eye of heaven shines,
And often is his gold complexion dimmed;
And every fair from fair sometime declines,
By chance, or nature's changing course, untrimmed;
But thy eternal summer shall not fade
Nor lose possession of that fair thou ow'st,
Nor shall Death brag thou wand'rest in his shade
When in eternal lines to time thou grow'st.
    So long as men can breathe or eyes can see,
    So long lives this, and this gives life to thee.

William Shakespeare

Activity:
1. a) Count the number of lines in each sonnet.
   b) Count the number of strong beats in each line.
   c) Describe the rhyme scheme.
   d) Divide the poem into sections according to principal ideas or images. Discuss the relationship of the sections.
   e) Based on your investigations, formulate a general statement about the nature of the sonnet. Confirm the accuracy of your statement by referring to the glossary on page 255.

Aeronaut to his Lady

I
    Through
    Blue
Sky
Fly
    To
    You.
Why?

Sweet
      Love,
Feet
    Move
      So
      Slow!

Frank Sidgwick

Question:
1. *Is this a sonnet? How do you know?*

Activities:
1. *Look for other sonnets in this book. Make a list of their similarities or differences.*
2. *Write a sonnet.*

Strawberry Haiku

• • • • •
• • • • • • •
The twelve red berries

Richard Brautigan

Question:
1.   Is this a haiku? How do you know?

Activity:
1.   Quickly scan this book and find as many haiku as possible.
Choose one haiku to read to the class, then analyze and discuss
the traits of haiku.

Siege

he peeps	i duck
i shoot	he ducks
i wave	he waves back
i peep	he shoots
he waves	i shoot
and duck	i peep

i peep again

he's dead

              draped across his turret

he smiles   my arrow tickles

the inside of his head

Johnny Byrne

Questions:
1. Why did the poet set up his poem in two columns?
2. As you read across the columns of the poem from left to right, where does the structure change? How and why does it change?

Activities:
1. Write a narrative about two people, using only two-word clauses.
2. Dramatize "Siege." Dramatize your own narrative.

Analysis of Baseball

It's about
the ball,
the bat,
and the mitt.
Ball hits
bat, or it
hits mitt.
Bat doesn't
hit ball, bat
meets it.
Ball bounces
off bat, flies
air, or thuds
ground (dud)
or it
fits mitt.

Bat waits
for ball
to mate.
Ball hates
to take bat's
bait. Ball
flirts, bat's
late, don't
keep the date.
Ball goes in
(thwack) to mitt,
and goes out
(thwack) back
to mitt.

Ball fits
mitt, but
not all
the time.
Sometimes
ball gets hit
(pow) when bat
meets it,
and sails
to a place
where mitt
has to quit
in disgrace.
That's about
the bases
loaded,
about 40,000
fans exploded.

It's about
the ball,
the bat,
the mitt,
the bases
and the fans.
It's done
on a diamond,
and for fun.
It's about
home, and it's
about run.

May Swenson

Questions:
1. Is this an accurate analysis of baseball?
2. Does the form of the poem add anything to the analysis?

Activity:
1. Write an explanation of a game or sport for someone who is
    unfamiliar with it.

Fortune

Fortune
has its cookies to give out

which is a good thing

since it's been a long time since

that summer in Brooklyn
when they closed off the street
one hot day
and the

FIREMEN

turned on their hoses

and all the kids ran out in it

in the middle of the street

and there were

maybe a couple dozen of us

out there

with the water squirting up

to the

sky

and all over
us

there was maybe only six of us
                                        kids altogether
                    running around in our
                                        barefeet and birthday
                    suits
                    and I remember Molly but then
        the firemen stopped squirting their hoses
            all of a sudden and went
                    back in
            their firehouse
                and
            started playing pinochle again
                    just as if nothing
                    had ever
                        happened
while I remember Molly
                        looked at me and

    ran in

because I guess really we were the only ones there

Lawrence Ferlinghetti

Activity:
1. *Rewrite this poem as a paragraph with conventional sentence
   structure and punctuation. Which version do you prefer? Why?*

12 NARRATIVE

"Tell them tell it to them"

Digging for China

"Far enough down is China," somebody said.
"Dig deep enough and you might see the sky
As clear as at the bottom of a well.
Except it would be real—a different sky.
Then you could burrow down until you came
To China! Oh, it's nothing like New Jersey.
There's people, trees, and houses, and all that,
But much, much different. Nothing looks the same."

I went and got the trowel out of the shed
And sweated like a coolie all that morning,
Digging a hole beside the lilac-bush,
Down on my hands and knees. It was a sort
Of praying, I suspect. I watched my hand
Dig deep and darker, and I tried and tried
To dream a place where nothing was the same.
The trowel never did break through to blue.

Before the dream could weary of itself
My eyes were tired of looking into darkness,
My sunbaked head of hanging down a hole.
I stood up in a place I had forgotten,
Blinking and staggering while the earth went round
And showed me silver barns, the fields dozing
In palls of brightness, patens growing and gone
In the tides of leaves, and the whole sky china blue.
Until I got my balance back again
All that I saw was China, China, China.

Richard Wilbur

Questions:
1. How old do you think the poet was when he tried digging for
   China?
2. a) What emotion does the poet experience as he writes the last
      line?
   b) In what ways have his perceptions of himself and his
      environment been changed?

Activities:
1. a) Explain why children dig.
   b) List the sequence of physical and mental activities generated
      by the act of digging.
2. Write a narrative, either in prose or verse, about an event in your
   childhood that changed your perceptions about yourself and your
   world.

Game After Supper

This is before electricity,
it is when there were porches.

On the sagging porch an old man
is rocking. The porch is wooden,

the house is wooden and grey;
in the living room which smells of
smoke and mildew, soon
the woman will light the kerosene lamp.

There is a barn but I am not in the barn;
there is an orchard too, gone bad,
its apples like soft cork
but I am not there either.

I am hiding in the long grass
with my two dead cousins,
the membrane grown already
across their throats.

We hear crickets and our own hearts
close to our ears;
though we giggle, we are afraid.

From the shadows around
the corner of the house
a tall man is coming to find us:

He will be an uncle,
if we are lucky.

Margaret Atwood

Questions:
1. *Why is the poet so precise in her description of the setting?*
2. *What is the "game"?*
3. *What is the significance of the final line?*

Activity:
1. *Write a short narrative poem about a game you played after supper as a child. Include as many specific details as possible.*

Aunt Sarah Died One Summer Night

Aunt Sarah died on a wicker chair on the porch one
    summer night with a cold lemonade and a Japanese
    fan and a dozen night bugs dancing around the 60
    watt bulb.

While the crickets chattered in the lawn,
    and the dog scratched and bit at his fur
    and the big black horsefly buzzed around the
    ceiling in our hot sticky kitchen.

While Mat and I kicked off our sneakers
    and ran over the wet grass, grabbing at the night
    for fireflies.

While Ma and Pa were driving to town
    in the green vegetable truck that smelt like
    tomatoes.

While Mary and her beau sat under the silver
    maple with leaves as big as hands, just watching the
    sky and saying nothing.

While the bullfrogs hidden in the cattails
    belched from swelling up with too much
    summer air.

Aunt Sarah died and the wind stroked her white curls,
    and a thrush perched on the highest branch sang
    her very favorite song, and the moon shone bright
    so she wouldn't stumble going up the golden
    stairs to heaven.

Lisa Hirschboeck

Questions:
1. What do you know about Aunt Sarah from the first and last stanzas?
2. What can be inferred about Aunt Sarah from stanzas 2 through 6?
3. Is the tone of this poem appropriate to the event described in it?

Activity:
1. Write a composition which recounts Aunt Sarah's thoughts on the night of her death.

The Sleeper

When I was the sissy of the block who nobody wanted
        on their team
Sonny Hugg persisted in believing that my small size
        was an asset
Not the liability and curse I felt it was
And he saw a use for my swift feet with which I ran
        away from fights.

He kept putting me into complicated football plays
Which would have been spectacular if they worked:
For instance, me getting clear in front and him
        shooting the ball over —
Or the sensation of the block, the Sleeper Play
In which I would lie down on the sidelines near the
        goal
As though resting and out of action, until the
        scrimmage began
And I would step onto the field, receive the long
        throw
And to the astonishment of all the tough guys in the
        world
Step over the goal line for a touchdown.

That was the theory anyway. In practice
I had the fatal flaw of not being able to catch
And usually had my fingers bend back and the
        breath knocked out of me
So the plays always failed, but Sonny kept on trying
Until he grew up out of my world into the glamorous
Varsity crowd, the popular kids of Lynbrook High.

But I will always have this to thank him for:
That when I look back on childhood
(That four psychiatrists haven't been able to help me
        bear the thought of)
There is not much to be glad for
Besides his foolish and delicious faith

That, with all my oddities, there was a place in the
     world for me
If only he could find the special role.

Edward Field

Questions:
1. *Why does the poet remember Sonny Hugg? What feelings does he have for Sonny?*
2. *What has happened to the poet since Sonny Hugg "grew up out of my world into the glamorous/Varsity crowd"?*

For Discussion
3. *What do you think it would be like to be "the sissy of the block"?*

Activities:
1. *Describe a friend whom you idolized in childhood.*
2. *Describe an incident or a plan that looked spectacular in theory but crumbled in practice.*

Flannan Isle

Though three men dwell on Flannan Isle
To keep the lamp alight,
As we steered under the lee we caught
No glimmer through the night.

A passing ship at dawn had brought
The news, and quickly we set sail,
To find out what strange thing might ail
The keepers of the deep-sea light.

The winter day broke blue and bright
With glancing sun and glancing spray
While o'er the swell our boat made way,
As gallant as a gull in flight.

But as we neared the lonely Isle
And looked up at the naked height,
And saw the lighthouse towering white
With blinded lantern that all night
Had never shot a spark
Of comfort through the dark,
So ghostly in the cold sunlight
It seemed, that we were struck the while
With wonder all too dread for words.
And, as into the tiny creek
We stole, beneath the hanging crag
We saw three queer black ugly birds —
Too big by far in my belief
For cormorant or shag —
Like seamen sitting bolt-upright
Upon a half-tide reef:
But as we neared they plunged from sight
Without a sound or spirt of white.

And still too mazed to speak,
We landed and made fast the boat
And climbed the track in single file,
Each wishing he were safe afloat
On any sea, however far,
So it be far from Flannan Isle:
And still we seemed to climb and climb
As though we'd lost all count of time
And so must climb for evermore;

Yet all too soon we reached the door—
The black sun-blistered lighthouse door
That gaped for us ajar.

As on the threshold for a spell
We paused, we seemed to breathe the smell
Of limewash and of tar,
Familiar as our daily breath,
As though 'twere some strange scent of death;
And so yet wondering side by side
We stood a moment still tongue-tied,
And each with black foreboding eyed
The door ere we should fling it wide
To leave the sunlight for the gloom:
Till, plucking courage up, at last
Hard on each others' heels we passed
Into the living-room.

Yet as we crowded through the door
We only saw a table spread
For dinner, meat and cheese and bread,
But all untouched and no one there;
As though when they sat down to eat,
Ere they could even taste,
Alarm had come and they in haste
Had risen and left the bread and meat,
For at the table-head a chair
Lay tumbled on the floor.

We listened, but we only heard
The feeble cheeping of a bird
That starved upon its perch;
And, listening still, without a word
We set about our hopeless search.
We hunted high, we hunted low,
And soon ransacked the empty house:
Then o'er the Island to and fro
We ranged, to listen and to look
In every cranny, cleft or nook
That might have hid a bird or mouse:
But though we searched from shore to shore
We found no sign in any place,
And soon again stood face to face
Before the gaping door,
And stole into the room once more

As frightened children steal.
Aye, though we hunted high and low
And hunted everywhere,
Of the three men's fate we found no trace
Of any kind in any place
But a door ajar and an untouched meal
And an overtoppled chair.

And as we listened in the gloom
Of that forsaken living-room —
A chill clutch on our breath —
We thought how ill-chance came to all
Who kept the Flannan Light,
And how the rock had been the death
Of many a likely lad —
How six had come to a sudden end
And three had gone stark mad,
And one, whom we'd all known as friend,
Had leapt from the lantern one still night
And fallen dead by the lighthouse wall —
And long we thought
On the three we sought,
And on what might yet befall.

Like curs a glance has brought to heel
We listened, flinching there,
And looked and looked on the untouched meal
And the overtoppled chair.
We seemed to stand for an endless while,
Though still no word was said,
Three men alive on Flannan Isle
Who thought on three men dead.

Wilfrid Wilson Gibson

Questions:
1. Which elements of the narrative create suspense?
2. How do rhythm and rhyme move the narrative along?
3. How do you account for the emotions the three men experience at the end of the poem?

Creation

And God stepped out on space,
And He looked around and said,
"I'm lonely—
I'll make me a world."

And as far as the eye of God could see
Darkness covered everything,
Blacker than a hundred midnights
Down in a cypress swamp.

Then God smiled,
And the light broke,
And the darkness rolled up on one side.
And the light stood shining on the other,
And God said, "That's good."

Then God reached out and took the light in His hands,
And God rolled the light around in His hands
Until He made the sun;
And He set that sun a-blazing in the heavens.
And the light that was left from making the sun
God gathered it up in a shining ball
And flung it against the darkness,
Spangling the night with the moon and stars.
Then down between
The darkness and the light
He hurled the world;
And God said, "That's good."

Then God himself stepped down—
And the sun was on His right hand
And the moon was on His left:
The stars were clustered about His head,
And the earth was under His feet.
And God walked, and where He trod
His footsteps hollowed the valleys out
And bulged the mountains up.

Then He stopped and looked and saw
That the earth was hot and barren.
So God stepped over to the edge of the world
And He spat out the seven seas;
He batted His eyes, and the lightnings flashed;
He clapped His hands, and the thunders rolled;
And the waters above the earth came down,
The cooling waters came down.

Then the green grass sprouted,
And the little red flowers blossomed,
The pine tree pointed his finger to the sky,
And the oak spread out his arms,
The lakes cuddled down in the hollows of the ground,
And the rivers ran down to the sea;
And God smiled again,
And the rainbow appeared
And curled itself around His shoulder.

Then God raised His arm and He waved His hand
Over the sea and over the land,
And He said, "Bring forth! Bring forth!"
And quicker than God could drop His hand,
Fishes and fowls
And beasts and birds
Swam the rivers and the seas,
Roamed the forests and the woods,
And split the air with their wings.
And God said, "That's good!"

Then God walked around,
And God looked around
On all that He had made.
He looked at His sun,
And He looked at His moon,
And He looked at His little stars;
He looked on His world
With all its living things,
And God said, "I'm lonely still."

Then God sat down
On the side of a hill where He could think;
By a deep, wide river He sat down;
With His head in His hands,
God thought and thought,
Till He thought, "I'll make me a man!"

Up from the bed of the river
God scooped the clay;
And by the bank of the river
He kneeled Him down;
And there the great God Almighty
Who lit the sun and fixed it in the sky,
Who flung the stars to the most far corners of the night,

Who rounded the earth in the middle of His hand;
This great God,
Like a mammy bending over her baby,
Kneeled down in the dust
Toiling over a lump of clay
Till He shaped it in His own image;
Then into it He blew the breath of life,
And man became a living soul.
Amen. Amen.

James Weldon Johnson

Questions:
1. According to the poet, what is the nature of the relationship
    between people and God?
2. To what kind of audience is the poem addressed? How do you
    know?

Activities:
1. Prepare a dramatic reading of this poem, paying special attention
    to tone.
2. Write a poem narrating the creation of the world as you envision it
    to have been.

A Dirge

Tell them tell it to them
That we the children of Ashiagbor's house
Went to hunt; when we returned,
Our guns were pointing to the earth,
We cannot say it; someone say it for us.
Our tears cannot fall,
We have no mouths to say it with.
We took the canoe, the canoe with sandload
They say the hippo cannot overturn
Our fathers, the hippo has overturned our canoe
   We come home
Our guns pointing to the earth.
Our mother, our dear mother
Where are our tears, where are our tears.
Give us mouth to say it, our mother.
We are on our knees to you
We are still on our knees.

Kofi Awoonor

Question:
1. What can be inferred about the hunters' (a) status within the tribe, (b) self-esteem, (c) responsibilities within the tribe, and (d) feelings as they return?

Activities:
1. In one sentence, explain what happened during the hunt.
2. Compose a narrative in which you try to explain why you have failed at an important task.

Sacrifice of a Rainbow Trout

Suddenly, from the rocky spring
A trout hung, trembling, in the air,
A jewel to the morning sun:

And then upon the mossy banks,
Rainy with rainbows, up he leaped
And tumbled wildly in the grass.

I ran to catch him where my hook
Pinned him behind a crusted rock
And ripped his mouth and gills apart.

I pulled his foaming stomach clean
And washed my fingers in the spring
And sat down and admired him.

His sunlit scales upon my hands,
I wrapped his flesh in leaves of elm
And homeward, singing, carried him.

I stripped him of his ivory bones,
Then held him, shining, to the fire
And tongued his body to my own.

And that was the supper that I had
While my imagination fed
Its silver hook upon the world.

Joseph Langland

Activities:
For Groups
1. *Discuss how the following elements contribute to the narrative: (a) diction, (b) tone, (c) imagery, and (d) syntax.*
2. *Paying special attention to the last stanza of the poem, explain the significance of the title.*

The Witch of Coos

I stayed the night for shelter at a farm
Behind the mountain, with a mother and son,
Two old-believers. They did all the talking.

MOTHER. Folks think a witch who has familiar spirits
She could call up to pass a winter evening,
But won't, should be burned at the stake or something.
Summoning spirits isn't 'Button, button,
Who's got the button,' I would have them know.

SON. Mother can make a common table rear
And kick with two legs like an army mule.

MOTHER. And when I've done it, what good have I done?
Rather than tip a table for you, let me
Tell you what Ralle the Sioux Control once told me.
He said the dead had souls, but when I asked him
How could that be — I thought the dead were souls,
He broke my trance. Don't that make you suspicious
That there's something the dead are keeping back?
Yes, there's something the dead are keeping back.

SON. You wouldn't want to tell him what we have
Up attic, mother?

MOTHER. Bones — a skeleton.

SON. But the headboard of mother's bed is pushed
Against the attic door: the door is nailed.
It's harmless. Mother hears it in the night
Halting perplexed behind the barrier
Of door and headboard. Where it wants to get
Is back into the cellar where it came from.

MOTHER. We'll never let them, will we, son! We'll never!

SON. It left the cellar forty years ago
And carried itself like a pile of dishes
Up one flight from the cellar to the kitchen,
Another from the kitchen to the bedroom,
Another from the bedroom to the attic,
Right past both father and mother, and neither stopped it.
Father had gone upstairs; mother was downstairs.
I was a baby: I don't know where I was.

MOTHER. The only fault my husband found with me —
I went to sleep before I went to bed,

Especially in winter when the bed
Might just as well be ice and the clothes snow.
The night the bones came up the cellar-stairs
Toffile had gone to bed alone and left me,
But left an open door to cool the room off
So as to sort of turn me out of it.
I was just coming to myself enough
To wonder where the cold was coming from,
When I heard Toffile upstairs in the bedroom
And thought I heard him downstairs in the cellar.
The board we had laid down to walk dry-shod on
When there was water in the cellar in spring
Struck the hard cellar bottom. And then someone
Began the stairs, two footsteps for each step,
The way a man with one leg and a crutch,
Or a little child, comes up. It wasn't Toffile:
It wasn't anyone who could be there.
The bulkhead double-doors were double-locked
And swollen tight and buried under snow.
The cellar windows were banked up with sawdust
And swollen tight and buried under snow.
It was the bones. I knew them—and good reason.
My first impulse was to get to the knob
And hold the door. But the bones didn't try
The door; they halted helpless on the landing,
Waiting for things to happen in their favor.
The faintest restless rustling ran all through them.
I never could have done the thing I did
If the wish hadn't been too strong in me
To see how they were mounted for this walk.
I had a vision of them put together
Not like a man, but like a chandelier.
So suddenly I flung the door wide on him.
A moment he stood balancing with emotion,
And all but lost himself. (A tongue of fire
Flashed out and licked along his upper teeth.
Smoke rolled inside the sockets of his eyes.)
Then he came at me with one hand outstretched,
The way he did in life once; but this time
I struck the hand off brittle on the floor,
And fell back from him on the floor myself.
The finger-pieces slid in all directions.
(Where did I see one of those pieces lately?
Hand me my button-box—it must be there.)
I sat up on the floor and shouted, 'Toffile,
It's coming up to you.' It had its choice

Of the door to the cellar or the hall.
It took the hall door for the novelty,
And set off briskly for so slow a thing,
Still going every which way in the joints, though,
So that it looked like lightning or a scribble,
From the slap I had just now given its hand.
I listened till it almost climbed the stairs
From the hall to the only finished bedroom,
Before I got up to do anything;
Then ran and shouted, 'Shut the bedroom door,
Toffile, for my sake!' 'Company?' he said,
'Don't make me get up; I'm too warm in bed.'
So lying forward weakly on the handrail
I pushed myself upstairs, and in the light
(The kitchen had been dark) I had to own
I could see nothing. 'Toffile, I don't see it.
It's with us in the room though. It's the bones.'
'What bones?' 'The cellar bones—out of the grave.'
That made him throw his bare legs out of bed
And sit up by me and take hold of me.
I wanted to put out the light and see
If I could see it, or else mow the room,
With our arms at the level of our knees,
And bring the chalk-pile down. 'I'll tell you what—
It's looking for another door to try.
The uncommonly deep snow has made him think
Of his old song, *The Wild Colonial Boy*,
He always used to sing along the tote road.
He's after an open door to get outdoors.
Let's trap him with an open door up attic.'
Toffile agreed to that, and sure enough,
Almost the moment he was given an opening,
The steps began to climb the attic stairs.
I heard them. Toffile didn't seem to hear them.
'Quick!' I slammed to the door and held the knob.
'Toffile, get nails.' I made him nail the door shut
And push the headboard of the bed against it.
Then we asked was there anything
Up attic that we'd ever want again.
The attic was less to us than the cellar.
If the bones liked the attic, let them have it.
Let them stay in the attic. When they sometimes
Come down the stairs at night and stand perplexed
Behind the door and headboard of the bed,
Brushing their chalky skull with chalky fingers,
With sounds like the dry rattling of a shutter,

That's what I sit up in the dark to say—
To no one any more since Toffile died.
Let them stay in the attic since they went there.
I promised Toffile to be cruel to them
For helping them be cruel once to him.

SON. We think they had a grave down in the cellar.

MOTHER. We know they had a grave down in the cellar.

SON. We never could find out whose bones they were.

MOTHER. Yes, we could too, son. Tell the truth for once.
They were a man's his father killed for me.
I mean a man he killed instead of me.
The least I could do was to help dig their grave.
We were about it one night in the cellar.
Son knows the story: but 'twas not for him
To tell the truth, suppose the time had come.
Son looks surprised to see me end a lie
We'd kept all these years between ourselves
So as to have it ready for outsiders.
But tonight I don't care enough to lie—
I don't remember why I ever cared.
Toffile, if he were here, I don't believe
Could tell you why he ever cared himself....

She hadn't found the finger-bone she wanted
Among the buttons poured out in her lap.
I verified the name next morning: Toffile.
The rural letter box said Toffile Lajway.

Robert Frost

Questions:
1. Why was the man killed?
2. What were the bones trying to do?
3. Why did the mother keep a finger bone in the button box?
4. What conclusions can you draw about the character and behaviour of (a) Toffile, (b) the mother, (c) the son, and (d) the narrator?
5. In what ways does the tone of the poem conform with what you expect in a "ghost" story? How does it differ?

Activities:
1. In point form, list the details of the mother's story.
2. Quote at least three descriptions of the bones.
3. Narrate the story from the point of view of either Toffile or the bones.

13 DESCRIPTIVE

"...wild orchids of the sea."

Recipe

Take a roof of old tiles
a short while after midday.

Place nearby
a fullgrown linden
stirred by the wind.

Above them put
a blue sky washed
by white clouds.

Let them be.
Watch them.

Eugene Guillevic

Question:
1. For what is the poem a "recipe"?

Activity:
1. Read the poem aloud. Now read the first three stanzas aloud
    without the verbs. Comment on the differences between the two
    readings.

Sea-Gulls

For one carved instant as they flew,
The language had no simile —
Silver, crystal, ivory
Were tarnished. Etched upon the horizon blue,
The frieze must go unchallenged, for the lift
And carriage of the wings would stain the drift
Of stars against a tropic indigo
Or dull the parable of snow.
Now settling one by one
Within green hollows or where curled
Crests caught the spectrum from the sun,
A thousand wings are furled.
No clay-born lilies of the world
Could blow as free
As those wild orchids of the sea.

E.J. Pratt

Activities:
1. *Compare the first line of "Sea-Gulls" with the first line of "Two Eagles" (opposite).*
2. *Compare the use of simile, metaphor, adjectives, and verbs in both poems. Which poem do you think is the most effective in its use of these techniques? Why?*

Two Eagles

Like white jade or a piece of cloud he stands
Throughout the clarity of autumn light.
This peerless, royal eagle countermands
All that the hunters do for his afright.
He mocks their nets; sharp arrows cannot bite
His sides; his proud and ever-dauntless soul
Scorns on the falconer's armlet to alight;
He frightens the huge roc, his royal goal,
Not the frail, timorous rabbit scurrying to a hole.

His mightier partner, a black eagle, flies.
I hardly believed there could be such a bird!
Perhaps he issues from the arctic skies?
Surely, no falconer has ever heard
Of such a one! At night his wings have stirred
The airs of the Sun Terrace. Geese and daws
Have fled in terror. His vast wings have whirred
High on the peaks of Wu. All birds must pause
Dreading his golden eyes and those white, fearful claws!

Unknown Chinese

Spring Breeze

You can't see it or hear it,
It is so soft. But it is strong enough
To dust the mirror with pollen,
And thrum the strings of the lute.

Ho Hsun

Question:
1. How does the poet manage to describe something that he can
    neither see nor hear?

Activity:
1. Devise a means by which you could see the wind. Describe what
    you see.

Pleasant Sounds

The rustling of leaves under the feet in woods and under hedges;
The crumping of cat-ice and snow down wood-rides, narrow
  lanes, and every street causeway;
Rustling through a wood or rather rushing, while the wind
  halloos in the oak-top like thunder;
The rustle of birds' wings startled from their nests or flying
  unseen into the bushes;

The whizzing of larger birds overhead in a wood, such as crows,
  puddocks, buzzards;
The trample of robins and woodlarks on the brown leaves, and
  the patter of squirrels on the green moss;
The fall of an acorn on the ground, the pattering of nuts on the
  hazel branches as they fall from ripeness;
The flirt of the groundlark's wing from the stubbles — how
  sweet such pictures on dewy mornings, when the dew
  flashes from its brown feathers!

John Clare

Questions:
1. What qualities of the sounds does the poet find pleasant?
2. What is the importance of the time of day?
3. a) Why does the author use so many phrases?
    b) What is the most descriptive word in each phrase?
4. What is the most beautiful-sounding word that you know?

Plowing

In afternoon the sun dips down the west
And wind-blown shadows dance beneath the trees' hem,
While, cracking the clods as it folds them,
A coulter lays bare the glass smooth frost.

The soil turned over on the hillock's breast
Spreads tobacco tints among the stubble there,
And the woodland, on which the light falls fair,
With this brown in red-gay hues is interlaced.

Sometimes a slowly wheeling crow takes note
Of an earthworm in the thinly furrowed ground
Near the unbleached grass, and drops down to prey.

And when the plowman turns his team around
Down near the elm tree, his plow emits a ray
That flashes blue like a starling's throat.

Alfred DesRochers

Activities:
1. *List all the words in the poem that suggest a colour without
   actually stating it.*
2. *List the words that establish the time of day and the season of the
   year.*
3. *Imagine that you are a professional photographer. Photograph this
   scene first in black and white, then in colour. Write a composition
   that explains the effects achieved by each photograph.*

Winter Uplands

The frost that stings like fire upon my cheek,
The loneliness of this forsaken ground,
The long white drift upon whose powdered peak
I sit in the great silence as one bound;
The rippled sheet of snow where the wind blew
Across the open fields for miles ahead;
The far-off city towered and roofed in blue
A tender line upon the western red;
The stars that singly, then in flocks appear,
Like jets of silver from the violet dome,
So wonderful, so many and so near,
And then the golden moon to light me home;
The crunching showshoes and the stinging air,
And silence, frost and beauty everywhere.

Archibald Lampman

Questions:
1. What is the predominant mood of the poem?
2. What images create the mood?
3. How does the mood of this poem compare with the mood of "Plowing," (opposite).

Activity:
1. Describe a familiar scene which instills in you a deeply felt mood. Use vivid images to convey the mood.

Portrait

Book-thin behind the desk
with fingers rigid as pencils she stamps
stacks returns, read or unread
she cares not.
Bloodless as paper she, and lifeless
as dead words on dull binding are her eyes,
looking not in or out only seeing
date-print on card and flyleaf;
and mute
as volumes never off the shelves her tongue —
the rubbered pencil used to point
the novel overdue the scanty fine.

O life — love — something — burst the resisting doors —
ignore the silence sign — vault the tall desk
and on her locked blank pages
write a living tale.

Anne Marriott

Questions:
1. What is a portrait?
2. What features determine the excellence of a portrait?
3. How does the poet use comparisons to portray the librarian?

Activity:
1. Using a descriptive technique similar to the author's, produce a
    portrait of someone you know.

Before Two Portraits of my Mother

I love the beautiful young girl of this
portrait, my mother, painted years ago
when her forehead was white, and there was no
shadow in the dazzling Venetian glass

of her gaze. But this other likeness shows
the deep trenches across her forehead's white
marble. The rose poem of her youth that
her marriage sang is far behind. Here is

my sadness: I compare these portraits, one
of a joy-radiant brow, the other care-
heavy: sunrise — and the thick coming on

of night. And yet how strange my ways seem,
for when I look at these faded lips my heart
smiles, but at the smiling girl my tears start.

Émile Nelligan
(translated by George Johnston)

Questions:
1. *What two images are presented in the poem?*
2. *What are the poet's responses to the images? How do you account
    for the conflicting responses?*

Activity:
1. *Find two photographs of yourself, one old and one recent.
    Compose a poem based on the two "likenesses."*

Portrait of a Girl With Comic Book

Thirteen's no age at all. Thirteen is nothing.
It is not wit, or powder on the face,
Or Wednesday matinee, or misses' clothing,
Or intellect, or grace.
Twelve has its tribal customs. But thirteen
is neither boys in battered cars nor dolls,
Not *Sara Crewe* or movie magazine,
Or pennants on the walls.

Thirteen keeps diaries and tropical fish
(A month, at most); scorns jumpropes in the spring;
Could not, would fortune grant it, name its wish;
Wants nothing, everything;
Has secrets from itself, friends it despises;
Admits none of the terrors that it feels;
Owns a half a hundred masks but no disguises;
And walks upon its heels.

Thirteen's anomalous — not that, not this:
Not folded bud, or wave that laps a shore,
Or moth proverbial from the chrysalis.
Is the one age defeats the metaphor.
Is not a town, like childhood, strongly walled
But easily surrounded, in no city.
Nor, quitted once, can it be quite recalled —
Not even with pity.

Phyllis McGinley

Question:
1. a) What is the difference between a mask and a disguise?
   b) Why does Thirteen own "a half a hundred masks but no disguises"?

Activities:
1. a) Define the word "anomalous."
   b) List everything that is anomalous about being thirteen, as presented in the poem.
   c) Make a list of anomalous features of the age thirteen that the poet does not mention.
2. Write a composition about the "ideal" age.

14 LYRIC

"...write the words love and loneliness"

Quiet Water

Quiet, only tiny ripples.
A fallen leaf drifts,
Following the wind-driven water.
A dragon-fly slowly settles
On the barely-moving leaf.
Dragon-fly-skipper on a ship of leaf
You sail calmly straight by.

As if the soul were that calm,
Weakly surrendering to this world
Without a protesting motion, not fighting its loneliness,
As if satisfied — and with just this.
And everything will always be just this way,
Only the muddy soil sinking invisibly deeper.

Samiati Alisjahbana
(translated by Burton Raffel and Nurdin Salam)

Questions:
1. What attracts the poet to the dragon-fly?
2. What does the poet disclose about herself in the second stanza?
3. Why does the poet wish that her soul were like the dragon-fly?

Activity:
1. Write a poem about satisfaction or dissatisfaction.

The Secret

Two girls discover
the secret of life
in a sudden line of
poetry.

I who don't know the
secret wrote
the line. They
told me

(through a third person)
they had found it
but not what it was,
not even

what line it was. No doubt
by now, more than a week
later, they have forgotten
the secret,

the line, the name of
the poem. I love them
for finding what
I can't find,

and for loving me
for the line I wrote,
and for forgetting it
so that

a thousand times, till death
finds them, they may
discover it again, in other
lines,

in other
happenings. And for
wanting to know it,
for

assuming there is
such a secret, yes,
for that
most of all.

Denise Levertov

Questions:
1. At what point in the poem does the poet stop describing the event and begin describing her reaction to it?
2. What is the poet's principal feeling for the two girls?
3. How would you account for the poet's feelings for two girls whom she has never met?

Activity:
1. Write a composition about why it is so hard to keep a secret.

The Six Strings

The guitar
makes dreams cry.
The crying of lost
souls
escapes from its round
mouth.
And like the tarantula
it weaves a huge star
to catch sighs
that float on its black
wooden tank.

Federico Garcia Lorca
(translated by Donald Hall)

Questions:
1. Can dreams cry? How can a guitar make dreams cry?
2. Can a tarantula weave a huge star? How can a guitar weave a huge star?
3. How can a guitar "catch sighs"? Can you "catch sighs"? How?

Activity:
1. Find a recording of Spanish guitar music. Listen to one selection on the record and describe what it conveys to you.

Eight Puppies

Between the thirteenth and the fifteenth day
the puppies opened their eyes.
Suddenly they saw the world,
anxious with terror and joy.
They saw the belly of their mother,
saw the door of their house,
saw a deluge of light,
saw flowering azaleas.

They saw more, they saw all,
the red, the black, the ash.
Scrambling up, pawing and clawing
more lively than squirrels,
they saw the eyes of their mother,
heard my rasping cry and my laugh.

And I wished I were born with them.
Could it not be so another time?
To leap from a clump of banana plants
one morning of wonders—
a dog, a coyote, a deer;
to gaze with wide pupils,
to run, to stop, to run, to fall,
to whimper and whine and jump with joy,
riddled with sun and with barking,
a hallowed child of God, his secret, divine servant.

                    Gabriela Mistral
              (translated by Doris Dana)

Questions:
1. Why do you think the poet wished to be born with the puppies?
2. In what sense is a puppy "a hallowed child of God"?
3. In what sense is a puppy God's "secret, divine servant"?

A lyric is a short, subjective poem with a songlike outburst of the author's innermost thoughts and feelings.

Activity:
1. Write a lyric poem about an experience that filled you with "terror and joy."

A Quoi Bon Dire

Seventeen years ago you said
    Something that sounded like Good-bye;
    And everybody thinks that you are dead,
        But I.

    So I, as I grow stiff and cold
To this and that say Good-bye too;
    And everybody sees that I am old
        But you.

    And one fine morning in a sunny lane
Some boy and girl will meet and kiss and swear
    That nobody can love their way again
        While over there
You will have smiled, I shall have tossed your hair.

Charlotte Mew

Questions:
1. What happened to the poet's lover seventeen years ago?
2. In the second stanza, what happens to the poet as she says "Good-bye"?
3. Where is "over there"?
4. What connection is there between the young couple and the old couple?

Activity:
1. a) Copy out lines 1, 2, 5, 6, 9, 10, and 11. Read these lines aloud as a unit.
   b) Copy out lines 3, 4, 7, 8, 12, and 13. Read these lines aloud as a unit.
   c) Comment on the relationship between the first and second set of lines.

Let My Last Breath Be Immortal Sandals:

for My Children

Let me die with the memory of their love songs in my ears —
their laughter, their anger, their tears,
sighing their full-breath't longings for my love —
let me die with their love songs in my ears.

Let my last breath be immortal sandals for their feet,
let my lungs give a last gift from my flesh:
let my throat sing its last sparrow-song for their fruition:
let my last breath be immortal sandals for their feet.

Lance Jeffers

Questions:
1. As he dies, what does the poet want from his children?
2. At the same time, what does the poet want to give to his children?
3. In what ways would their "love songs" differ from his "sparrow-song"?

Activities:
1. Explain what you would do with a pair of "immortal sandals."
2. In a brief essay, describe the relationship you would like to have with your own children.

Night

Night
The silence of night
Flows around me
Like enormous undersea currents.

I lie on the bottom of dumb, green water.
I hear my heart
Sending its light and dark signals
Like a lighthouse.

A voiceless rhythm
A secret code
I decipher no mysteries.

At each flash of light
I close my eyes
To keep the continuity of darkness
The endlessness of the silence
Engulfing me.

Anne Hébert

Questions:
1. *How do the comparisons in the poem establish its mood?*
2. *Why does the poet want "To keep the continuity of darkness/The endlessness of the silence/Engulfing me."?*

Activity:
1. *Write a poem entitled "Night Thoughts."*

The Plowman

All day I follow
Watching the swift dark furrow
That curls away before me,
And care not for skies or upturned flowers,
And at the end of the field
Look backward
Ever with discontent.

A stone, a root, a strayed thought
Has warped the line of that furrow—
And urge my horses round again.

Sometimes even before the row is finished
I must look backward;
To find, when I come to the end
That there I swerved.

Unappeased I leave the field,
Expectant, return.

The horses are very patient.
When I tell myself
This time
The ultimate unflawed turning
Is before my share,
They must give up their rest.

Someday, someday, be sure,
I shall turn the furrow of all my hopes
But I shall not, doing it, look backward.

Raymond Knister

Questions:
1. *Why does the plowman have problems in keeping his furrows straight?*
2. *What aspects of the plowman's character demand that his furrow be straight?*
3. *What is the poet saying in the last stanza?*

Activities:
1. *Using an extended metaphor, write a poem about being a student.*
2. *Write a short essay explaining what society expects of you as a student.*

Your Country

If you open your eyes
If you put your hands
On snow, birds, trees, and animals
Patiently, gently
With your whole heart's weight;

If you take time by the hand
And if you look at the soil
Patiently, gently;

If you recognize these men
If you recognize the grief
Which trembles in the depths of their eyes;

If you write the words love and loneliness
Patiently, gently,
On every season, on every house;

If you give a name to blood, bread, day, night
And that fierce and exact flame
Which burns in the heart of everything;

If you embrace every death of your childhood
Patiently, gently,
With all the weight of your despair:

Then your country will be born.

Gatien Lapointe

Questions:
1. *What country is the poet writing about?*
2. *Where is "your country"?*
3. *Has the poet stated all of the conditions necessary to give your country life?*

Activities:
1. *Write a poem about your country.*
2. *Go back to the poem in this book that has meant the most to you. Write a poem in response to the one you have chosen.*

Glossary

Alliteration
The repetition of an initial sound in two or more words of a phrase, line of poetry, or sentence.

Anachronism
An error in chronology placing an event, person, item, or language expression in the wrong period.

Concrete Poetry
Poetry which depends in part upon the arrangement of words and letters to convey meaning.

Diction
The style of speaking and writing as reflected in the choice and use of words. Diction refers both to the selection of words in statements and to the accuracy, emphasis, and distinction with which they are spoken and written.

Epigram
A witty, ingenious, and pointed saying that is expressed tersely.

Epitaph
A brief poem or other form of writing praising a deceased person.

Haiku
A form of Japanese verse usually employing allusions and comparisons. A haiku is composed of three lines containing a fixed number of syllables, usually seventeen.

Image
The mental impression or visualized likeness summoned up by a word, phrase, or sentence.

Irony
A device in which the literal meaning of a word or statement is the opposite of that intended.

Lyric
A short, subjective poem with a songlike outburst of the author's innermost thoughts and feelings.

Metaphor
A figure of speech in which a word or phrase is applied to a person, idea, or object to which it is not literally applicable. A metaphor is an implied analogy which imaginatively identifies one thing with another.

Onomatopoeia
The formation and use of words that suggest by their sounds the object or idea being named.

Personification
A figure of speech in which abstractions, animals, ideas, and inanimate objects are endowed with human form, character, traits, or sensibilities.

Rhyme
Similarity or identity of sound in words.

Simile
A figure of speech in which two things, essentially different but thought to be alike in one or more respects, are compared.

Sonnet
A poem of fourteen lines, usually in iambic pentameter, with rhymes arranged according to certain definite patterns (rhyme schemes). A sonnet usually expresses a single, complete thought, idea, or sentiment.

Syntax
The arrangement of words into phrases, clauses, and sentences.

Tone
An author's attitude or point of view toward his or her subject.

Index of Titles

Index of Authors

Index of Themes

ADOLESCENCE

ANIMALS

CHILDHOOD

DEATH

IDEAS

LOVE

MACHINES

MYSTERY

Acknowledgements

Grateful acknowledgement is made to publishers and owners of copyrighted material for permission to reprint the selections listed.

The dedication quotation on page xiii is reprinted by permission of Farrar, Straus and Giroux, Inc. Excerpt from "To Acario Cotapos" from *Fully Empowered* by Pablo Neruda, translated from the Spanish by Alistair Reid. Translation copyright © 1967, 1969, 1970, 1975 by Alistair Reid. Also reprinted by permission of Souvenir Press Ltd., London.

1 SOUND

P. 4: Rod Wilmot's "Listening" appeared first in his *Haiku* (1969), and subsequently in *The Haiku Anthology* (1974). **P. 5:** "Church Bells, Montreal" is reprinted from *Collected Poems of Raymond Souster* by permission of Oberon Press. **P. 6:** "The Watch" is reprinted from *Collected Poems by Frances Cornford*. Reprinted by permission of Cresset Press, part of the Hutchinson Publishing Group, England. **P. 7:** Dylan Thomas, *Under Milk Wood*. Copyright 1954 by New Directions Publishing Corporation. All rights reserved. Reprinted by permission of New Directions and David Higham Associated Limited. **P. 8:** Reprinted with permission of Macmillan Publishing Co., Inc., from *Collected Poems of Vachel Lindsay* (New York: Macmillan, 1925). **P. 10:** "Dog Around the Block" from *The Fox of Peapack and Other Poems* by E.B. White. Reprinted by permission of Harper & Row, Publishers, Inc. **P. 12:** Reprinted with permission of Macmillan Publishing Co., Inc., from *Collected Works by Vachel Lindsay*. Copyright 1920 by Macmillan Publishing Co., Inc., renewed 1948 by Elizabeth C. Lindsay, **P. 16:** The Society of Authors on behalf of the copyright owner Mrs. Iris Wise. **P. 16:** Reprinted with permission of Macmillan Publishing Co., Inc. Copyright 1916 by Macmillan Publishing Co., Inc. Renewed by James Stephens. **P. 18:** Reprinted by permission of Faber and Faber Ltd. from *Wodwo* by Ted Hughes. Copyright © 1967 by Ted Hughes. Reprinted by permission of Harper & Row, Publishers, Inc. **P. 19:** From *Good Morning, America,* copyright 1928, 1956 by Carl Sandburg. Reprinted by permission of Harcourt Brace Jovanovich, Inc.

2 SIMILE

P. 23: "At a mantis," "Like a conclusion," "After a heated argument" (**P. 38**), and "With a crunching sound" (**P. 64**) translated by Makoto Ueda and reprinted from *Modern Japanese Haiku: An Anthology* by Makoto Ueda, by permission of University of Toronto Press © University of Toronto Press 1976. **P. 24:** From *Sappho: A New Translation* by Mary Barnard. Copyright 1957 by The Regents of the University of California. Reprinted by permission of the University of California Press. **P. 25:** Federico Garcia Lorca, *Selected Poems*. Copyright © Herederos de Federico Garcia Lorca 1954. **P. 26:** From *There's a Trick with a Knife I'm Learning to Do*: Poems 1963-1978, by Michael Ondaatje (McClelland & Stewart) 1980 © Michael Ondaatje. Also reprinted with the permission of W.W. Norton & Company, Inc. Copyright © 1979. **P. 28:** Author of *The Warp*, a poetic novel in three volumes published by Sphere, London. **P. 29:** The estate of the late Edna St. Vincent Millay. **P. 30:** From *A Tropical Childhood and Other Poems* by Edward Lucie-Smith © Oxford University Press 1961. **P. 31:** "The Other Morning," "Bride" (**P. 52**), and "Twilight Entered My Room" (**P. 125**) copyright © 1973 Kimon Friar. The Lantz Office Incorporated, 888 Seventh Avenue, New York, New York, 10106, Agent. **P. 32:** Henri Coulette, "The Black Angel," in *The War of the Secret Agents and Other Poems*. Copyright © 1966 by Henri Coulette. (New York: Charles Scribner's Sons, 1966). Reprinted with the permission of Charles Scribner's Sons.

3 METAPHOR

P. 37: "The Flame" is reprinted from *Collected Poems of Raymond Souster* by permission of Oberon Press. **P. 38:** "Searching on the wind," "Moon fades..." (**P. 73**), "The stillness of dawn" (**P. 89**) from *The Zen Haiku of J.W. Hackett* (original title: *The Way of Haiku*).

Tokyo: Japan Publications, Inc., © 1983; distributed by Kodansha International and Harper & Row. Reprinted by permission of J.W. Hackett. **P. 42:** Reprinted by permission of the author. **P. 45:** From *Times Three* by Phyllis McGinley. Copyright © 1955 by Phyllis McGinley. Originally published in *The New Yorker*. Reprinted by permission of Viking Penguin Inc. and Martin Secker & Warburg Limited. **P. 46:** From *The Poems of Stanley Kunitz*, by Stanley Kunitz. © 1978 by Stanley Kunitz. First appeared in *The Atlantic*. By permission of Little, Brown and Company in association with the Atlantic Monthly Press. **P. 47:** From *Poems: New & Selected*, published by Oxford University Press. By permission of the author.

4 PERSONIFICATION

P. 51: Mrs. Nicolete Gray and The Society of Authors on behalf of the Laurence Binyon Estate. **P. 53:** From *Roots and Wings*, edited by Hardie St. Martin: "Time, Give Me the Secret" by Juan Ramón Jiménez, translated by Ralph Nelson and Rita Garcia Nelson. Copyright © 1976 by Hardie St. Martin. Reprinted by permission of Harper & Row, Publishers, Inc. **P. 54:** P.W.H. Harvey for "November" from *Gloucestershire* by F.W. Harvey. **P. 55:** From *Roots and Wings*, edited by Hardie St. Martin: "Death of a Pair of Shoes" by Jorge Guillen, translated by Philip Levine. Copyright © 1976 by Hardie St. Martin. Reprinted by permission of Harper & Row, Publishers, Inc. **P. 56:** © Copyright 1962 Kenneth Koch. **P. 57:** Reprinted by permission of Faber and Faber Ltd. from *Wodwo* by Ted Hughes. "Thistles" from *Selected Poems* by Ted Hughes. Copyright © 1961 by Ted Hughes. Reprinted by permission of Harper & Row, Publishers, Inc. **P. 58:** Reprinted by permission of Russell & Volkening, Inc. as agents for the author. Copyright © 1943 by Kenneth Fearing, renewed 1971. Also reprinted by permission of Harcourt Brace Jovanovich, Inc. from *Afternoon of a Pawnbroker*, copyright 1943, 1971 by Kenneth Fearing.

5 IMAGERY

P. 63: "If you are squeamish," "Standing by my bed" (**P. 73**), and "Pain penetrates" (**P. 78**) from *Sappho: A New Translation* by Mary Barnard. Copyright © 1958. Reprinted by permission of University of California Press, publisher. **P. 65:** From *Song at the Years Turning* by R.S. Thomas. Reprinted by permission of Granada Publishing Limited. **P. 66:** "The Delicately Sloping Neck" by Miguel de Unamuno, English translation by Hardie St. Martin from *Roots and Wings*: Poetry from Spain 1900-1975 by Hardie St. Martin. Copyright © 1976 by Hardie St. Martin. Reprinted by permission of Harper & Row, Publishers, Inc. **P. 67:** From *Facing the Tree* by David Ignatow. First appeared in the *Hawaii Review*. By permission of Little, Brown and Company in association with the Atlantic Monthly Press. **P. 68:** Reprinted by permission of Faber and Faber Ltd. from *Advice to a Prophet* by Richard Wilbur. Also reprinted by permission of Harcourt Brace Jovanovich, Inc. **P. 69:** Copyright © 1962 by Karl Shapiro. Reprinted from *Selected Poems* by Karl Shapiro, by permission of Random House, Inc. Originally appeared in *The New Yorker*. **P. 70:** "Child on Top of a Greenhouse" copyright 1946 by Editorial Publications, Inc. from *The Collected Poems of Theodore Roethke* by Theodore Roethke. Reprinted by permission of Doubleday & Company, Inc. Also reprinted by permission of Faber and Faber Ltd. from *The Collected Poems of Theodore Roethke*. **P. 71:** Reprinted from *The Massachusetts Review*, © 1974, The Massachusetts Review, Inc. **P. 72:** Copyright © 1962 by *Saturday Review*. All rights reserved. Reprinted by permission. **P. 73:** From *The Complete Poems of Paul Lawrence Dunbar* by Paul Lawrence Dunbar. By permission of Dodd, Mead & Company, Inc. **PP. 74-75:** Both these poems and "Birth" (**P. 164**), "By Way of Error" (**P. 175**) from *The Poetry of Modern Quebec*, Fred Cogswell, Editor & Translator, Montreal, Harvest House Ltd., 1976. **P. 76:** From *Poems: New and Selected*, published by Oxford University Press. Reprinted by permission of the author. **P. 77:** To Messrs. Faber and Faber Ltd., publishers of *Collected Poems* by Edward Thomas, and to Myfanwy Thomas. **P. 79:** Mrs. Nicolete Gray and The Society of Authors on behalf of the Laurence Binyon Estate. **P. 80:** William Carlos Williams, *Pictures from Brueghel*. Copyright © 1962 by William Carlos Williams. Reprinted by permission of New Directions Publishing Corporation. **P. 81:** From *Collected Earlier Poems*. Copyright 1938 by New Directions Publishing Corporation. Reprinted by permission of New Directions. **P. 82:** Reprinted by permission of Farrar, Straus and Giroux, Inc. From *Elizabeth Bishop: The Complete Poems*. Copyright © 1940, 1969 by Elizabeth Bishop. **P. 84:** From *An Almanac for Twilight*, by Jack Matthews. (The University of North Carolina Press, 1966) Copyright 1966 Jack Matthews. Reprinted by permission of the publisher.

6 DICTION

P. 90: From Kenneth Rexroth, *One Hundred More Poems From the Chinese*. Copyright © 1970 by Kenneth Rexroth. Reprinted by permission of New Directions Publishing Corporation. **P. 91:** Copyright © 1961 by The Antioch Review, Inc. First printed in *The Antioch Review*, Vol. 20, No. 4 (Winter 1960–61). Reprinted by permission of the Editors. **P. 93:** From *The Collected Poems of Howard Nemerov*. The University of Chicago Press, 1977. Reprinted by permission of the author. **P. 96:** From *100 Selected Poems* by e.e. cummings. Reprinted by permission of Granada Publishing Ltd. Also reprinted from *Complete Poems 1913-1962* by e.e. cummings, by permission of Harcourt Brace Jovanovich, Inc. Copyright 1944 by E.E. Cummings; renewed 1972 by Nancy T. Andrews. **P. 98:** "Alligator on the Escalator" from *Catch a Little Rhyme* by Eve Merriam. Published by Atheneum. Copyright © 1966 by Eve Merriam. Reprinted by permission of the author. **P. 99:** Copyright © 1961 by Robert Penn Warren. Reprinted by permission of the William Morris Agency, Inc. on behalf of the author. Copyright © 1966 by Robert Penn Warren. Reprinted from *Or Else: Poem/Poems 1968-1974*, by Robert Penn Warren, by permission of Random House, Inc. **P. 102:** From *The Poems of Stanley Kunitz 1928-1978* by Stanley Kunitz. © 1978 by Stanley Kunitz. By permission of Little, Brown and Company in association with the Atlantic Monthly Press.

7 SYNTAX

P. 107: From *The Second Life* by Edwin Morgan. Reprinted by permission of Edinburgh University Press. **P. 110:** Copyright © 1948 by Robert Francis. Reprinted from *The Orb Weaver* by permission of Wesleyan University Press. This poem first appeared in *Forum*. **P. 113:** "Foul Shot" by Edwin A. Hoey from *Read* magazine, a Xerox Education Publication. Copyright © 1962. Reprinted by permission of Xerox Education Publications. **P. 114:** From New and Collected Poems 1917–1976 by Archibald MacLeish. Copyright © 1976 by Archibald MacLeish. Reprinted by permission of Houghton Mifflin Company. **P. 116:** Copyright © 1963 by Vassar Miller. Reprinted from *My Bones Being Wiser* by permission of Wesleyan University Press. **P. 117:** "Spring is like a perhaps hand" is reprinted from *Tulips and Chimneys* by e.e. cummings, by permission of Liveright Publishing Corporation. Copyright 1923, 1925 and renewed 1951, 1953 by E.E. Cummings. Copyright © 1973, 1976 by The Trustees for the E.E. Cummings Trust. Copyright © 1973, 1976 by George James Firmage. From *Complete Poems 1913-1962* by e.e. cummings. Reprinted by permission of Granada Publishing Limited. **P. 118:** From *New & Selected Things Taking Place* by May Swenson. © 1963 by May Swenson. First appeared in *The Hudson Review*. By permission of Little, Brown and Company in association with the Atlantic Monthly Press. **P. 120:** "Les parents exemplaires" by Éloi de Grandmont. First published in *Chardon à foulon écrits de Canada Français*, Montreal, 1963.

8 MOOD

P. 127: Mary Panegoosho Cousins, 1962, Ottawa, Ontario. **P. 128:** From *Facing the Tree* by David Ignatow. © 1973 by David Ignatow. First appeared in *The Nation*. By permission of Little, Brown and Company in association with the Atlantic Monthly Press. **P. 129:** From *Stella Benson: Poems* by Stella Benson. Reprinted by permission of Mrs. G. Berkeley, copyright holder. **P. 130:** From *French Poetry Today* by Jacques Prévert, edited by Simon Watson Taylor © 1971. Reprinted by permission of André Deutsch, London, England. **P. 133:** © 1961 by John Moffitt. Reprinted from his volume *The Living Seed* by permission of Harcourt Brace Jovanovich, Inc. **P. 134:** Reprinted with permission of Faber and Faber Ltd. from *Collected Poems* by George Barker. **P. 135:** "Girl with 'Cello" is reprinted from *A Grain of Mustard Seed*, New Poems by May Sarton, with the permission of W.W. Norton & Company, Inc. Copyright © 1971 by May Sarton. Reprinted by permission of Russell & Volkening as agents for the author. Copyright © 1971 by May Sarton. **P. 136:** Reprinted by permission of the author.

9 TONE

P. 141: From Ms. Joseph's collection, *Rose in the Afternoon*, first published by J.M. Dent and Sons Ltd. in 1974. Reprinted by permission of John Johnson, Authors' Agents, England. **P. 142:** Reprinted by permission of A.D. Peters and Co. Ltd. **P. 143:** By permission of the author. **P. 144:** From *The Poems of Catullus*, trans. © Peter Whigham (Penguin Classics, 1966) p. 197. Reprinted by permission of Penguin Books Ltd. **P. 145:** From *Collected Poems by Frances Cornford*. Reprinted by permission of Cresset Press, part of the Hutchinson Publishing Group, London, England. **P. 146:** Sandra Abma, Grade 9, Garson Falconbridge High School. Reproduced by permission of Methuen Publications, 161 Eglinton Ave. East, Toronto. **P. 147:** Both these poems and "Lament" (**P. 152**) courtesy of The Estate of the late Edna St. Vincent Millay. **P. 149:** Copyright © 1953 by *Saturday Review*. All rights reserved. Reprinted by permission. **P. 150:** Reprinted by permission of Arnoldo Mondadori Editore, S.p.a., Milan, **P. 151:** By permission of the author. **P. 153:** From *Selected Poems* by Yevgeny Yevtushenko, trans. Robin Milner-Gulland and Peter Levi (Penguin Modern European Poets, 1962) p. 52. Copyright © Robin Milner-Gulland and Peter Levi, 1962. Reprinted by permission of Penguin Books Ltd. **P. 154:** From *Children of Albion: Poetry of the Underground in Britain* by Patrick Waites, Editor Michael Horovitz. **P. 155:** "Last Lesson of the Afternoon" from *The Complete Poems of D.H. Lawrence*. Copyright © 1964, 1971 by Angelo Ravagli and C.M. Weekley, Executors of the Estate of Frieda Lawrence Ravagli. Used by permission of Viking Penguin Inc. Also by permission of Laurence Pollinger Ltd. and the Estate of Mrs. Frieda Lawrence Ravagli. **P. 156:** From *New Statesman*, November 15, 1968, by Frances Gill.

10 IRONY

P. 161: From Gunnar Harding and Anselm Hollo, editors *Modern Swedish Poetry in Translation*. University of Minnesota Press, Minneapolis. Copyright © 1979 by the University of Minnesota. **P. 162:** From *Versus* by Ogden Nash. Copyright 1949 by Ogden Nash. By permission of Little, Brown and Company. Also reprinted by permission of Curtis Brown, Ltd. Copyright © 1948 by Ogden Nash © renewed 1976 by Isabel Nash Eberstadt and Linell Nash Smith. **P. 163:** Reprinted by permission of the publishers and the trustees of Amherst College from *The Poems of Emily Dickinson*, by Emily Dickinson, edited by Thomas H. Johnson, Cambridge, Mass.: The Belknap Press of Harvard University Press, Copyright 1951, © 1955, 1979 by the President and Fellows of Harvard College. **P. 165:** From *170 Chinese Poems* translated by Arthur Waley. Reprinted by permission of Constable Publishers, England. From *Translations from the Chinese*, translated by Arthur Waley. Copyright 1919 and renewed 1947 by Arthur Waley. Reprinted by permission of Alfred A. Knopf, Inc. Reprinted by permission of George Allen & Unwin, England. **P. 167:** Both this poem and "Digging for China" (**P. 211**) reprinted by permission of Faber and Faber Ltd. From *Poems 1943–1956* by Richard Wilbur. **P. 167:** Copyright © 1952 by The New Yorker Magazine, Inc.; renewed 1980 by Richard Wilbur. Reprinted from his volume Things of This World, by permission of Harcourt Brace Jovanovich, Inc. **P. 168:** From *Selected Poems* by Miroslav Holub, trans. Ian Milner and George Theiner (Penguin Modern European Poets, 1967) p. 21. Copyright © Miroslav Holub, 1967; translation copyright © Penguin Books Ltd., 1967. Reprinted by permission of Penguin Books Ltd. **P. 169:** By F.R. Scott, reprinted by permission of the Canadian Publishers, McClelland and Stewart Limited, Toronto. **P. 171:** "The Adversary" from *Times Three* by Phyllis McGinley. Copyright © 1959 by Phyllis McGinley. Originally published in *The New Yorker*. Reprinted by permission of Viking Penguin Inc. **P. 172:** Reprinted by permission of Farrar, Straus and Giroux, Inc. from *Poems 1965-1975* by Seamus Heaney. Copyright © 1966, 1980 by Seamus Heaney.

Reprinted by permission of Faber and Faber Ltd. from *Death of a Naturalist* by Seamus Heaney. **P. 173:** Reprinted by permission of Faber and Faber Ltd. from *Collected Poems* by W.H. Auden. Copyright 1940 and renewed 1968 by W.H. Auden. Reprinted from *W.H. Auden: Collected Poems*, by W.H. Auden, edited by Edward Mendelson, by permission of Random House, Inc. **P. 174:** From *French Poetry Today*, by Raymond Queneau, edited by Simon Watson Taylor © 1971. Reprinted by permission of André Deutsch, England. **P. 176:** Copyright © 1953 by Robert Francis. Reprinted from *The Orb Weaver* by permission of Wesleyan University Press. "Pitcher" first appeared in *New Poems by American Poets I*. **P. 177:** Copyright © 1967 by Paul Goodman. Reprinted from *Collected Poems*, by Paul Goodman, edited by Taylor Stoehr, by permission of Random House Inc.

11 FORM

P. 183: "She Loves Me" by Emmett Williams, from *Anthology of Concretism*, (ed.) Eugene Wildman. (Chicago: Swallow Press, 1969). **P. 184:** Reprinted from *Visual Language*, by Richard Kostelanetz (Assembling Press, 1970), by permission of the author (P.O. Box 73, Canal St., New York, NY 10013). Copyright © 1968, 1970 by Richard Kostelanetz. **P. 188:** Reprinted with permission December 1968 issue *Yale Alumni Magazine*. © Yale Alumni Publications. **P. 190:** Reprinted by arrangement with the Estate of Harry Chapin. **P. 192:** From *Flowers in Concrete* by Mary Ellen Solt. © 1966 by Indiana University Press. Reprinted by permission of Indiana University Press. **P. 194:** "Sweethearts" by Emmett Williams from *Concrete Poetry: A World View*. © 1965. Reprinted by permission of Indiana University Press, Publisher. **P. 196:** From *Our Ground Time Here Will be Brief* by Maxine Kumin. Copyright © 1982 by Maxine Kumin. Reprinted by permission of Viking Penguin Inc. **P. 198:** From *The Poetry of Robert Frost*, edited by Edward Connery Lathem. Copyright 1942, © 1962 by Robert Frost. Copyright © 1969 by Holt, Rinehart and Winston. Copyright © 1970 by Lesley Frost Ballantine. Reprinted by permission of Holt, Rinehart and Winston, Publishers. **P. 199:** From *The Poetry of Robert Frost*, edited by Edward Connery Lathem. Reprinted by permission of the Estate of Robert Frost and Jonathan Cape Ltd., England. **P. 203:** By permission of the author. **P. 205:** From *New & Selected Things Taking Place* by May Swenson. © 1971 by May Swenson. By permission of Little, Brown and Company in association with the Atlantic Monthly Press. **P. 206:** From *A Coney Island of the Mind* by Lawrence Ferlinghetti. Copyright © 1958 by Lawrence Ferlinghetti. Reprinted by permission of New Directions Publishing Corporation.

12 NARRATIVE

P. 211: From *Things of This World*, © 1956 by Richard Wilbur. Reprinted by permission of Harcourt Brace Jovanovich, Inc. Reprinted by permission of Faber & Faber Ltd. from *Poems 1943-1956* by Richard Wilbur. **P. 212:** From *Procedures for Underground* by Margaret Atwood © Oxford University Press Canada. Also by permission of Little, Brown and Company in association with the Atlantic Monthly Press. **P. 213:** Reprinted by permission of Scholastic Writing Awards Program. Copyright 1978 by Scholastic Inc. **P. 214:** Reprinted by permission of Grove Press, Inc. Copyright © 1963 by Edward Field. **P. 216:** From *Collected Poems* by W.W. Gibson. By permission of Mr. Michael Gibson and Macmillan, London and Basingstoke. **P. 219:** "Creation" from *God's Trombones* by James Weldon Johnson. Copyright 1927 by The Viking Press, Inc. Copyright Renewed by Grace Nail Johnson. Reprinted by permission of Viking Penguin Inc. **P. 222:** From *Messages: Poems from Ghana* by Kofi Awoonor and Adali-Mortty. Copyright © 1971 by Kofi Awoonor and Adali-Mortty. Reprinted by permission of Heinemann Educational Books, London. **P. 223:** © Joseph Langland, from *The Wheel of Summer*, Dial 1963. **P. 224:** From *The Poetry of Robert Frost*, edited by Edward Connery Lathem. Copyright 1923, © 1969 by Holt, Rinehart and Winston. Copyright 1951 by Robert Frost. Reprinted by permission of Holt, Rinehart and Winston, Publishers. Also reprinted by permission of Jonathan Cape Ltd. on behalf of the Estate of Robert Frost.

13 DESCRIPTIVE

P. 231: Eugene Guillevic, *Selected Poems*. Copyright © 1968, 1969 by Denise Levertov Goodman and Eugene Guillevic. Reprinted by permission of New Directions Publishing

Corporation. **P. 232:** Reprinted by permission of University of Toronto Press. **P. 233:** Reproduced by permission of the publishers from *Ancient Poetry from China, Japan, and India*, rendered into English verse by Henry W. Wells. Copyright © 1968 by the University of South Carolina Press. **P. 234:** Ho Hsun, ed. Kenneth Rexroth, *One Hundred More Poems from the Chinese*. Copyright © 1970 by Kenneth Rexroth. Reprinted by permission of New Directions Publishing Corporation. **P. 235:** From *A Book of Peace* by Elizabeth Goudge. Published by Michael Joseph Ltd., London. **P. 236** and **P. 239:** From *The Poetry of Modern Quebec*, edited and translated by Fred Cogswell, Montreal, Harvest House, 1976 ("French Writers of Canada" Series). **P. 240:** "Portrait of a Girl With Comic Book" from *Times Three* by Phyllis McGinley. Copyright 1952 by Phyllis McGinley. Copyright renewed 1980 by Julie Elizabeth Hayden and Phyllis Hayden Blake. Originally published in *The New Yorker*. Reprinted by permission of Viking Penguin Inc. Also reprinted by permission of Martin Secker & Warburg Limited, London.

14 LYRIC

P. 245: From *Anthology of Modern Indonesian Poetry*, edited and translated by Burton Raffel and Nurdin Salam. © 1962, 1963, 1964. Reprinted by permission of State University of New York Press. **P. 246:** Denise Levertov, *O Taste and See*. Copyright © 1964 by Denise Levertov Goodman. Reprinted by permission of New Directions Publishing Corporation. **P. 248:** Federico Garcia Lorca, *Selected Poems*. Copyright © Herederos de Federico Garcia Lorca 1954. **P. 249:** Reprinted by permission of Joan Daves. Copyright © 1961, 1964, 1970, 1971 by Doris Dana. **P. 250:** From *Collected Poems* by Charlotte Mew. Reprinted by permission of Gerald Duckworth & Co. Ltd. **P. 251:** Reprinted by permission of Broadside Press, Dudley Randall, Editor. **P. 252** and **P. 254:** From *The Poetry of Modern Quebec*, edited and translated by Fred Cogswell, Montreal, Harvest House, 1976 ("French Writers of Canada" Series). **P. 253:** From *The Collected Poems of Raymond Knister*. Reprinted by permission of McGraw-Hill Ryerson Limited. **P. 255:** Glossary definitions from *Concise Dictionary of Literary Terms* by Harry Shaw. © 1972 by McGraw-Hill Inc. Reprinted by permission of McGraw-Hill Inc.